English Vocabulary in Use

elementary

英语在用

剑桥初级英语词汇

Michael McCarthy (英)

Felicity O'Dell (英)

D1663009

外语教学与研究出版社
FOREIGN LANGUAGE TEACHING AND RESEARCH PRESS

剑桥大学出版社
CAMBRIDGE UNIVERSITY PRESS

(京)新登字 155 号

京权图字：01－2000－1675

图书在版编目（CIP）数据

剑桥初级英语词汇/（英）麦卡锡（McCarthy, M.），（英）奥德尔（O'Dell, F.）著．－北京：外语教学与研究出版社，2001

ISBN 7－5600－2148－4

Ⅰ.剑…　Ⅱ.①麦…②奥…　Ⅲ.英语－词汇　Ⅳ.H313

中国版本图书馆 CIP 数据核字(2001)第 00691 号

英语在用
剑桥初级英语词汇
原著：（英）Michael McCarthy
　　　（英）Felicity O'Dell
　　*　　　*　　　*
策划编辑：宋微微　任小玫
责任编辑：黄江岩
出版发行：外语教学与研究出版社
社　　址：北京市西三环北路 19 号（100089）
网　　址：http：//www.fltrp.com.cn
印　　刷：中国农业出版社印刷厂
开　　本：787×1092　1/16
印　　张：10.75
版　　次：2001 年 2 月第 1 版　2001 年 2 月第 1 次印刷
印　　数：1—10000 册
书　　号：ISBN 7－5600－2148－4/H·1140
定　　价：22.00 元
　　*　　　*　　　*
如有印刷、装订质量问题出版社负责调换

英语学习者的"圣经"
——"英语在用"丛书简介

一套全面、实用的语法和词汇参考书是几乎所有英语学习者的梦想。如今我们欣喜地告诉大家，随着"英语在用"丛书的出版，这个梦想可以实现了。

本丛书是世界上最畅销的英语语法与词汇学习参考书，迄今读者已逾千万，被誉为"英语学习者的'圣经'"。它专为非英语国家英语学习者编写，在结构上，条理明晰，形式简约顺达；在内容上，解析重点与难点，透彻生动，同时反复练习，巩固成效。

"英语在用"丛书包括语法和词汇两个系列，每系列分 3 级，分别针对初、中、高级学习者，并配有练习册。既可作为自学用书，也可作为课堂用书。

本丛书的特点是：

- **教法新颖**：以"在语境中学习语言"为原则，辅以大量生动的图表，摒弃死记硬背的陈旧方法。
- **内容实用**：取材自真实的语料库，强调内容的实用性，使您真正达到学以致用。
- **结构简明**：将语法和词汇项目分类解说，方便您挑选所需内容。
- **使用方便**：采用解说与练习左右两页对照的形式。左页解释说明语法规则和词汇意义，右页通过练习巩固本单元所学用法，随学随练，让您能每迈一步都体会到进步的成就感。
- **技巧训练**：介绍学习技巧，帮助您自己总结语法及词汇规律，养成良好的学习习惯。
- **参考答案**：详尽全面，给您充分的信息。
- **目　　录**：清晰详细，说明每单元讲解的词汇和语法，便于快速寻找所需内容。
- **索　　引**：将书中讲解的所有重要词汇和语法点按字母顺序列出，并标注书中位置，方便查找。
- **附　　录**：丰富全面，提供多方面的参考资料。

  语法附录包括：被动语态，引语，不规则动词，常见错误等。

  词汇附录包括：音标表，常用习语，常见错误等。

"英语在用"丛书原书由剑桥大学出版社出版。外语教学与研究出版社引进本套丛书，旨在介绍国际先进的英语学习方法，帮助学习者对英语融会贯通，学有卓效。《荀子》"劝学篇"中有一脍炙人口的佳句："吾尝终日而思矣，不如须臾之所学也；吾尝跂而望矣，不如登高之博见也。"又有："学而不化，非学也。"如果大家能藉此套丛书通达学路，登顶揽胜，我们便可聊以自慰了。

"英语在用"丛书将分英文版和中文注释版两种陆续出版。首批推出：

词汇部分：

- English Vocabulary in Use: elementary 剑桥初级英语词汇
- English Vocabulary in Use: pre-intermediate and intermediate 剑桥中级英语词汇
- English Vocabulary in Use: upper-intermediate and advanced 剑桥高级英语词汇

语法部分：

- Essential Grammar in Use 剑桥初级英语语法
- English Grammar in Use 剑桥中级英语语法
- Advanced Grammar in Use 剑桥高级英语语法
- Essential Grammar in Use Supplementary Exercises 剑桥初级英语语法练习
- English Grammar in Use Supplementary Exercises 剑桥中级英语语法练习

Contents

The world

At home

School and workplace

Leisure

Social issues

Acknowledgements

We would like to thank Gillian Lazar, Geraldine Mark and Stuart Redman for their invaluable reports on the initial manuscript. We are also grateful to the students and staff at various institutions who assisted in piloting the material in different parts of the world: Hülya Akgün, Özel Gökdil Lisesi, Istanbul, Turkey; Monika Barczyk, Sosnowiec, Poland; Anna Cerna, The Bell School, Prague, Czech Republic; Leigh Fergus, Paris, France; Sharon Hartle, Verona, Italy; Gary Hicks and David Parry, Embassy Language and Training Centre, Hove, England; Grazyna Kanska, Warsaw, Poland; Stephanie Lott, St. John's–Bell Language Centre, Bangkok, Thailand; Elena Marinina, Moscow State University, Moscow, Russia; Dr Miroslawa Modrzewska, Gdansk, Poland; Dr Ramzy Radwan, Cairo, Egypt; M G Rogers, English One, Seville, Spain; Margot Teschendorf, Melbourne, Australia.

Many thanks are due to Nóirín Burke of Cambridge University Press, who guided this book through the editorial process. She set the deadlines that motivated us to get the book done, and chased us when we lagged behind. Geraldine Mark, as usual, proved to be the most professional of editors when the typescript passed into her hands and made many useful comments that have improved the book. Ellen Shaw, who worked on the American edition of the upper-intermediate *English Vocabulary in Use*, has continued to offer sound advice which we hope is reflected at this level. Our domestic partners must always get a special thank-you for being so tolerant of the long hours we spend away from them in the company of our computer keyboards. Whatever faults and shortcomings remain in the book must be laid entirely at our door.

Michael McCarthy
Felicity O'Dell

Cambridge, January 1998

Introduction

To the student

This book has been written to help you learn new vocabulary. You already know hundreds of English words, but to speak and write English in normal situations you need at least 1–2,000 words. In this book, there are around 1,250 new words and phrases for you to learn. You will find them on the left-hand page of each unit. Every new word or phrase is used in a sentence, or in a conversation, or has a picture with it, or has some explanation of what it means. On the right-hand page there are exercises and other activities to help you practise using the words and to help you to remember them. The book has been written so that you can use it yourself, without a teacher. You can do the units in any order you like, but we believe it is a good idea if you do Units 1 and 2 first, as they will help you to work with the rest of the book in the best possible way.

The key at the end of the book is for you to check your answers to the exercises after you do them. The key sometimes has more than one answer. This is because often there is not just one correct way of saying something. The key also has possible answers for most of the exercises which are open-ended, or where you are asked to talk about yourself.

The index at the end of the book has all the important words and phrases from the left-hand pages. The index also tells you how to pronounce words. There is a table of phonetic symbols to help you understand the pronunciation on page 157.

You should also have a dictionary with you when you use the book. This is because sometimes you may want to check the meaning of something, or find a word in your own language to help you remember the English word. Sometimes, you will also need a dictionary for the exercises; we tell you when this is so.

To learn a lot of vocabulary, you have to do two things:

1 Study each unit of the book carefully and do all the exercises. Check your answers in the key. Repeat the units after a month, and then again after three months, and see how much you have learnt and how much you have forgotten. Repeating work is very important.

2 Develop ways of your own to study and learn new words and phrases which are not in this book. For example, every time you see or hear an interesting phrase, write it in a notebook, and write who said it or wrote it, and in what situation, as well as what it means. Here is an interesting example:

   ready: *(man at the door of a theatre, to all the people waiting)* 'Have your tickets ready please!' = have your ticket in your hand.

   Making notes of the situations words are used in will help you to remember them and to use them at the right moment.

We hope you like this book. When you have finished it, you can go to the next book in the series, *English Vocabulary in Use: pre-intermediate and intermediate*, and after that, to the higher level, *English Vocabulary in Use: upper-intermediate and advanced*.

To the teacher

This book can be used in class or as a self-study book. It is intended to take learners from a very basic level of vocabulary to a level where they can use around 2,000 words and phrases. The vocabulary has been chosen for its usefulness in everyday situations, and the authors consulted a written and spoken corpus of present-day English to help them decide on the words and phrases to be included. The new vocabulary (on average 20–25 items per unit) is presented with illustrations and explanations on the left-hand page, and there are exercises and activities on the right-hand page. There is a key and an index with pronunciation for all the key vocabulary.

The book focuses not just on single words, but on useful phrases and collocations. For example, difficult teaching points such as the difference between **do** and **make**, are dealt with through collocation (we **do** our homework, but we **make** mistakes), and useful phrases (e.g. **come along**, in the unit on **come**) are presented.

The book is organised around everyday topics, but also has units devoted to core verbs such as **get** and **bring/take**, as well as units concerned with ways of learning vocabulary. Typical errors are indicated where appropriate, and the most typical meanings and uses are focused on for each key item. The units in the book can be used in any order you like, but we would advise doing the initial units on learning vocabulary (Units 1 and 2) first, as these lay the foundations for the rest of the book.

The right-hand pages offer a variety of different types of activities, some traditional ones such as gap-filling, but also more open-ended ones and personalised activities which enable learners to talk about their own lives. Although the activities and exercises are designed for self-study, they can be easily adapted for pair-work, group-work or whole-class activities in the usual way. The key sometimes gives alternative answers to the exercises, and also usually gives possible model answers for the more personalised ones.

When the learners have worked through a group of units, it is a good idea to repeat some of the work (for example, the exercises) and to expand on the meaning and use of key words and phrases by extra discussion in class, and find other examples of the key items in other texts and situations. This can be done at intervals of one to three months after first working on a unit. This is important, since it is usually the case that a learner needs five to seven exposures to a word or phrase before they can really know it, and no single book can do enough to ensure that words are always learnt first time.

When your students have finished all the units in this book, they will be ready to move on to the two higher level books in this series: *English Vocabulary in Use: pre-intermediate and intermediate*, by Stuart Redman, and after that, to the higher level, *English Vocabulary in Use: upper-intermediate and advanced*, by the same authors as this book.

We hope you enjoy using the book.

1 Talking about language

A Language words

This book uses some grammar words in English.

grammar word	meaning	example	in your language
noun	a person or thing	book, girl, pen	
verb	something we do	do, read, write	
adjective	describes a person or thing	good, bad, happy, long	
adverb	describes a verb	slowly, badly	
preposition	a little word used before a noun or pronoun	in, on, by, at	
singular	just one	book, house	
plural	more than one	books, houses	
phrase	a group of words (*not* a complete sentence)	in a house, at home, an old man	
sentence	a complete idea in writing, beginning with a (capital letter) and ending with a (full stop)	(T)he man went into the room and closed the door	
paragraph	a short part of a text (one or more sentences) beginning on a new line	This book has 60 units. Each unit has 2 pages.	
dialogue	a conversation between two people	Ann: How's Jo? Bill: OK, thanks.	
question	a set of words that begin with a (capital letter) and end with a (question mark)	(A)re you English? Do you like school(?)	
answer	reply to a question	Yes, I am. No, I don't.	

B The language of the exercises in this book

Here are some of the instructions which we often use for the exercises.

1 Match the words on the left with the words on the right. Draw lines.
   orange ⟍⟋ ice-cream
   chocolate ⟋⟍ juice
2 Fill the gaps in the sentence.
   Jack is ....at...... home today.
3 Correct the mistakes in the sentences.
   Jack is ~~in~~ home today. *Jack is at home today.*
4 Complete the sentence for yourself.
   I go to work by ....bus.....
5 Add another example.
   cat, dog, horse,....cow...

Exercises

1.1   Write the grammar words in A opposite in your own language.

1.2   Look at B opposite. Write the exercise instructions in your own language.

1.3   Write these words in the correct column.

book speak good word house have
write new man right blue say

noun	*verb*	*adjective*
book		

1.4   Think of four examples of prepositions.

....

1.5   Are these phrases, sentences or questions?

1 in the park *phrase*
2 Do you speak English?
3 a black cat
4 She's writing a book.
5 What's your name?
6 I like English.

1.6   Answer these questions.

1 What is the plural of **book**?
2 What is the singular of **men**?
3 Is **from** a verb?
4 Is **cat** an adjective?
5 Is 'Jane loves Hari.' a phrase?
6 Is **bad** an adverb?

1.7   Follow these instructions.

1 Fill the gap in the question.   What ......*is*.... your name?
2 Add another example of a colour.   black, green, blue …
3 Correct these words.   speek, inglish
4 Answer this question.   Is there a river in your town?
5 Match the verbs on the left with the nouns on the right. Draw lines.

     make   homework
     do   a shower
     have   a mistake

2 Learning vocabulary

Here are some ways of writing down words you want to learn.

A Write down words that go together (collocations)

You **do the exercises** in this book. Sometimes, you may **make mistakes** in your English. In your vocabulary book, write down: **do an exercise** and **make a mistake**.

When words are used together like this, we call it a **collocation**.
You go **by train**, but **on foot** (= walking)   preposition + noun
Some people are **good at** languages [NOT good ~~in~~]   adjective + preposition
I saw a very **tall man** [NOT ~~high~~ man]   adjective + noun

B Learn words in families

word family	some words in the family
temperature	**hot, warm, cool, cold**
travel	**ticket, passport, suitcase**

C Pictures and diagrams

Draw pictures. For example: **car**

windscreen
boot
window
wheel
door
headlight

Draw diagrams like this one. Put more words in as you learn them.

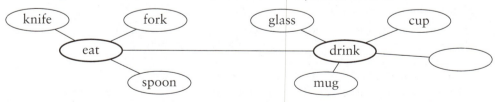

knife   fork   glass   cup
eat   drink
spoon   mug

Exercises

2.1 Look at Unit 3 of this book. How many more collocations for *have* could you write in your vocabulary notebook?

have a party, a shower ....

2.2 Which words can go with *weather*? Use a dictionary.

wet   high   big   dry   warm   happy   cool   rainy   dark

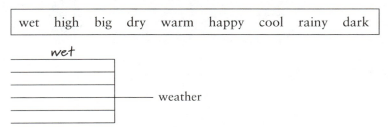

_____ wet
_____
_____ ———— weather
_____
_____

2.3 There are two word families here. What are they? Put them in the table. Use a dictionary.

school   rain   sun   teacher   cloud   exam   snow   ice   student

name of family	words in family

2.4 Draw simple pictures to help you remember these words, as in the example.

Example: **to cry**

1 a plane **lands**
2 **sunny weather**
3 **under** the table

2.5 Put words in the empty circles.

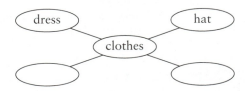

chair   desk
   furniture

dress   hat
   clothes

> **Tip:** Now make sure you have started a vocabulary notebook before you do the other units in this book.

3 Have/had/had

A **What can you have?**

You can ...
1 **have** lunch
2 **have** a party
3 **have** a lesson
4 **have** a cup of tea/coffee
5 **have** a shower /ˈʃaʊə/

B **Other things you can have**

	example	other things
1	lunch	dinner breakfast a meal something to eat
2	a party	a meeting a competition a game (of football/chess/cards)
3	a lesson	an exam homework an appointment (with the dentist)
4	tea/coffee	a drink a sandwich an ice-cream some cheese
5	a shower	a bath a swim a sauna

C **Expressions with have**

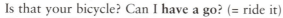

Is that your camera? Can I **have a look**?
    (= look at it)
Is that your bicycle? Can I **have a go**? (= ride it)
Goodbye! **Have a good journey!** (= somebody is going away)
Do you **have a moment**? (= have some time) Can **I have a word with you**? (= speak to you)
We always **have a good time** in our English lessons (= fun; we enjoy them)
I'm going to **have my hair cut**. See you later. Can you meet me at the hairdresser's?
I want to learn to ski but I **don't have the time**.

D **Have + got (speaking/informal) = have (writing/formal)**

I've **got** three sisters. **Have** you **got** any brothers and sisters?
My house is big. **It's got** five bedrooms and three bathrooms.
We've got ten minutes before the train goes.
Have you **got** a pen?
(*In a shop*) A: Do you sell postcards? B: Yes, but we **haven't got** any at the moment.
I've **got** a problem. Can I have a word with you?
I've **got** a cold / a headache. /ˈhedeɪk/

E **Have to**

We use **have to** when the situation means you **must** do something.
The museum's not free. You **have to** pay $10 to go in.
All students **have to** do the exam.
I haven't got a car, so I **have to** walk to school every day.

Exercises

3.1 **Fill the gaps in the sentences. Use words from A and B opposite.**

1 I always have .... (and ....) for breakfast.
2 I have an .... with the dentist at 3 o'clock.
3 Do you want to have a game of ....?
4 Jane's having a .... on Saturday. Are you going?
5 Do you want to have a ....? The bathroom's just here.
6 I have an .... tomorrow, so I have to study tonight.
7 We must have a .... to talk about these problems.
8 I'm going to the cafeteria to have a .... Do you want to come?
9 The hotel has a swimming pool, so we can have a .... every day.
10 We can have .... before the film, or we can eat after it.

3.2 **Answer the questions about *yourself*.**

1 Have you got any brothers or sisters?
2 What time do you have English lessons?
3 What do you have for lunch?
4 Do you have to go to lessons every day?
5 How many pens have you got with you now?
6 Do you always have a party on your birthday?
7 What do you usually have when you go to a restaurant?

3.3 **Do the crossword.**

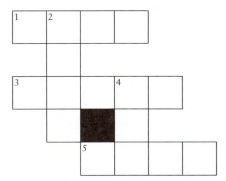

Across
1 You have it in a restaurant.
3 People often have one on their birthday.
5 Do you want to have a .... of tennis?

Down
2 You have it at school or university.
4 If you don't like coffee, you can have ....

3.4 **What do you say?**

1 (*Someone is thirsty*) Why don't you have ....?
2 (*Someone is going away*) Bye! Have a ....!
3 (*Someone sneezes* [*Atchoo!*] *and has a red nose*) Oh! have you got a ....?
4 (*Someone has a new camera*) Is that new? Can I have ....?

4 Go/went/gone

A Go

Go means to move from one place to another.

I **go** to work by bike. My brother **goes** by car.
We **went** to Paris last summer.
Shall we **go** to the swimming pool today?

You can go to a place on foot or in some kind of transport.
To make it clear that we are going on foot we can say:
We're **walking** to work this morning.

Is this train **going** to Granada?

Where **does** this road **go**?

A   B

B Go + prepositions

Kim **went in(to)** his room
and shut the door.

Yuko **went out of** the house
and **into** the garden.

Rani was tired. He **went up**
the stairs slowly.

The phone was ringing. She
went down the stairs quickly.

Go away.

I'm **going back** home this evening.
(See Unit 7.)

home

C Go + -ing for activities

Go is often used with **-ing** for different activities.

I hate **going shopping**.

I usually **go swimming**
in the morning.

Let's **go dancing**.

Do you like **going sightseeing**
when you are on holiday?

Hans **goes skiing**
every winter.

Bob is **going
fishing** today.

D Future plans

be going to is often used for plans for the future:

On Saturday Jan is **going to visit** his aunt. On Sunday we're **going to stay** at home. On
Monday I'm **going to meet** Sam at the restaurant.

Exercises

4.1 Where are these people going? Follow the lines.

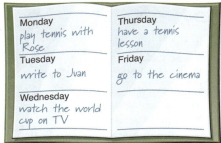

1 Pablo ...is going to the zoo...
2 Soraya and Mehmet ....
3 Imran ....
4 The Patels ....
5 Natasha ....

4.2 Correct the mistakes in these sentences.

1 Please, go ~~in~~ I'm tired.   ....away................................
2 We're going sightsee today.   ....
3 Jo went down to the top of the hill.   ....
4 Let's go to fish today.   ....
5 She went out off the shop.   ....

4.3 Look at the activities in C opposite. Which do you do on holiday? Write sentences.

I usually go shopping on holiday.

4.4 Write about Alison's plans for next week.

Monday play tennis with Rose	**Thursday** have a tennis lesson
Tuesday write to Juan	**Friday** go to the cinema
Wednesday watch the world cup on TV	

1 On Monday .....Alison is going to play tennis with Rose.......................
2 On Tuesday ....
3 On Wednesday ....
4 On Thursday ....
5 On Friday ....

4.5 Write about where trains, buses and roads go to from your town.

From Cambridge, trains go to London and to Norwich.

4.6 Look in a book in English. What examples of *go* can you find?

5 Do/did/done

A Do as auxiliary

questions   **Do** you **like** tennis?   **Did** they **like** the film?
short answers   Yes, I **do**.   Yes, they **did**.
                So **does** Sinjit.   So **did** I.
negatives   He **doesn't play** well.   Jo **didn't see** it.

B What are you doing?

Do as a general verb

What **do** you **do** to relax?
I listen to music.

Don't **do** that, Tommy.

What **are** the people in the picture **doing**?
They're dancing.

C What do you do?

What **do** you **do**? (= What is your job?)
I'm a student. *or* I'm a teacher. *or* I'm an engineer.

What **does** your wife **do**? (= What's your wife's job?)
She's a doctor. *or* She's a secretary. *or* She's a mechanic.

D Do + task

do the housework
do the gardening
do the washing
do the washing-up
do your homework
do some exercises
do business with
do your best

Did you **do the washing** this morning?
No, I'm going to **do** it later.

Our company **does a lot of business with** the USA.

The homework exercise is very difficult – just **do your best**.

Tip: Make a note of any expressions with **do** that you find when you are reading in English.

See Unit 6 for the contrast between **do** and **make**.

Exercises

5.1 Write questions and answers about the people in the picture.

1 (the boy) .... *What is the boy doing? He's eating an ice-cream.*

2 (the woman) ....

3 (the girls) ....

4 (the man in the house) ....

5 (the dog) ....

6 (the man in the garden) ....

5.2 Write questions and answers about the jobs of the people in the pictures.

1 Lee Atkins   2 Lara Brown   3 Sophie Hicks   4 Jo   Ted

1 .... *What does Lee Atkins do? He's a teacher.* ....

2 ....

3 ....

4 ....

5.3 Write questions about what the people in exercise 5.2 did this morning. Answer the questions using the phrases in the box.

| talk to five patients   ~~teach 3 lessons~~   write an essay   go to a meeting |

1 .... *What did Lee Atkins do? He taught three lessons.* ....

2 ....

3 ....

4 ....

5.4 Look at the *do* expressions in D. Write sentences about you or your family and these activities.

I do a lot of housework but I never do the gardening.

5.5 Correct the mistakes in this dialogue.

ANNA: Where did you went on your holidays? To London?

PAVEL: No, we don't go to London this year. We went to Scotland.

ANNA: Do your grandmother lives in Scotland?

PAVEL: No, she don't but my uncle do.

6 Make/made/made

Make ...

To **make coffee**.    To **make dinner**.

I'll **make some tea/hot chocolate**. /ˈtʃɒklət/
I **make breakfast/lunch/supper** every day. (supper = a meal just before bed)

B

Make a ...

The teacher's **making a photocopy**.

He's **making a film/video** of the class.

The children are **making a noise**.

C

Don't **make** mistakes with make!

Can I say ...?	yes/no	Correction
I **made** a mistake in the exercise.	✓	
I have to **make** my homework.	✗	I have to **do** my homework.
I have to **make** an exam next week.	✗	I have to **take/do** an exam next week.
When I get up I **make** my bed.	✓	
I want to **make** an appointment with the doctor. (= fix a time to see him/her)	✓	
I'd like to **make** a photo of you.	✗	I'd like to **take** a photo of you.
After dinner, I'll help you **make** the dishes.	✗	After dinner I'll help you **do** the dishes.

D

It **makes** me (feel) ...

Going by train always **makes me** (**feel**) tired.

My friend called me stupid. It **made me** (**feel**) angry.

That film **made me** (**feel**) sad.

English Vocabulary in Use (elementary)

Exercises

6.1 Fill the gaps with *make* or *do*.

1 I always .... a lot of mistakes when I speak English.
2 If I .... my homework every day, my English will get better.
3 Let's go to bed now. We can .... the dishes in the morning.
4 I want to .... an exam in French. Do you know where I can .... one?
5 We always try not to .... a noise after ten o'clock at night.

6.2 Complete the sentences with *make(s)/made me feel*.

1 That film .... sad.
2 Long lessons always .... tired.
3 She was horrible to me; it .... angry.

6.3 What are these people doing? Complete the sentences using *make*.

1 He's ....

3 The children are ....

2 She's ....

4 They're ....

6.4 Correct the mistakes in these sentences. Look at the example.

1 I have to ~~make~~ my homework. *I have to do my homework.*
2 Can I make a photo of you?
3 He's 25 but he never makes his own washing. He takes his dirty clothes to his mother's.
4 What do you think, yes or no? We must do a decision today.
5 I have to take an appointment with the doctor. Do you have her phone number?
6 I do mistakes when I speak English.
7 Are you making an exam tomorrow?

7 Come/came/come

Come and go are different:

HERE go THERE   HERE come THERE

A Come in/out

We say '**Come in!**' when someone knocks at the door of a room.
Then the person who knocked **comes into** the room.

Come out is often the opposite of **come in**.
A woman **came out of** the shop with
two big bags. (I was in the street.)

You put your money in and the ticket
comes out of the machine.

B Come back and come home

Come back means 'return to *this place here*'.
She went away for three days. She **came back** yesterday. (She is here again.)

Come back is often used with **from**.
They **came back from** Italy yesterday.

Come home is similar; 'home' is 'here' for the person speaking.

MOTHER: What time did you **come home** last night?
ANNE: Oh, about eleven o'clock.
MOTHER: What! Eleven! That's much too late!

C Other important uses of come

A: What country do you **come from**?
B: I'm from **Norway**. (*or* I **come from** Norway. *or* I'm Norwegian.)

We're going to a disco tonight. Do you want to **come along**? (= come with us)

Come and see me some time. (= visit me)

> **Tip:** Write down any prepositions you find with **come** every time you see them.

Exercises

7.1 **Fill the gaps in the sentences.**

1 I put money in, but the ticket didn't come ..*out of*... the machine.
2 A: I'm going to Taiwan tomorrow.
   B: Oh! When are you coming ....?
   A: Two weeks from now.
3 The teacher came .... the classroom and started the lesson.
4 A: Where do you come ....?
   B: I'm Brazilian.
5 Come and .... me at five o'clock; we can talk about it then.
6 The children come .... school at four o'clock.

7.2 **Answer these questions for *yourself*.**

1 What time do you come home every day?
2 What country do you come from?
3 What do you do when you come into your classroom?

7.3 **What do you think these people are saying?**

1 ....   3 ....

2 ....

7.4 **Fill the gaps using *come* in the correct form.**

1 Have you .... for your letters? They're on the table.
2 She .... back yesterday.
3 He .... here every Tuesday.
4 .... you .... to the school party tonight?

7.5 **Look up these verbs in a dictionary. Write the meaning in your vocabulary book. You may find more than one meaning, but just write down *one* meaning for each verb. After a week, cover the verbs, look at your notes and see if you can remember the verbs.**

1 come round   2 come across   3 come up

8 Take/took/taken

A Take with time (*it + take + person + time*)

It **takes** Alan 20 minutes to get to work.
Alan's house → 20 minutes → Alan's office

It **takes** Miriam 45 minutes to get to work.
Miriam's flat → 45 minutes → Miriam's office

I go to school/university every day. It **takes** me 30 minutes.
I do homework every day. It **took** /tʊk/ me two hours yesterday.

How long does it **take** to get to the station? 15 minutes in a taxi.

B Take with courses/exams, etc.

Are you **taking** an English course? Yes.
Do you have to **take** an exam? Yes, at the end of the course.
I want to **take** some Japanese lessons.

C Take with bus, car, etc.

How do you get to work? I **take** the bus.

In Paris you can **take** the metro to the Eiffel Tower.

How does Nik get to work?
He **takes** the train.

D Take something with you

Are you going out? **Take** an umbrella.
It's raining.

Are you going to the beach? **Take** some water with you.

Sorry, you can't **take** your camera
into the museum.

Useful expression: Can I **take a photograph** here? /ˈfəʊtəgræf/

> **Tip:** Make a page in your notebook for **take** and put in new words that go with it
> when you see them (e.g. a picture, a look at, a chance).

Exercises

8.1 Fill the gaps for yourself.

1 It .... me .... minutes to get to school/university.
2 It takes me .... minutes/hours to go from .... to ....
3 .... takes me .... to do one unit of this book.

8.2 Complete the sentences using *take/took* and an expression from the box.

| a course   your driving test   some lessons   an exam |

1 At the end of the course, you have to ....
2 I wanted to speak French, so I ....
3 You want to learn Russian? Why don't you ....?
4 In Britain, when you are 17, you can ....

8.3 Look at the pictures. Answer the questions using *take*.

1 How does Lisa go to work?
   She ....

3 How does Simon go to school?
   He ....

2 How can I get to the airport?
   You ....

4 How do Paul and Ann get home every day?
   They ....

8.4 What do you take with you when ...
1 you want to take photographs?

2 it's raining?

3 you go to another country?

4 you go to your English lessons?

8.5 How long did it take you to do this unit?

9 Bring/brought/brought

A Bring and take

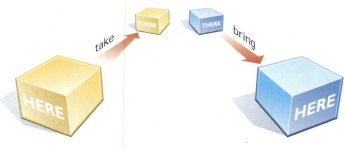

take = from *here* to *there*

bring = from *there* to *here*

Are you going to school? **Take** your books. (*from here* to the school)
Are you going to the kitchen? Can you **bring** me a glass? (from the kitchen *to here*)

Please **take** this form to the secretary. (the secretary is *there*)

Come to my house tomorrow and **bring** your guitar. (for me, my house is *here*)

B Bring somebody something

A: I've **brought** /brɔːt/ you some apples from my garden.
B: Oh, thank you!

When she visits me, she always **brings** me flowers.

C Bring something back

It's raining. You can **take** my umbrella and **bring** it **back** tomorrow.

TOM: This book is interesting.
ANN: Please **take** it with you and read it.
TOM: Thanks. I'll **bring** it **back** on Friday.
ANN: OK. No problem.

Exercises

9.1 Fill the gaps with *take* or *bring*.

1 Are you going to the shops? ....Take........ an umbrella. It's raining.
2 'Don't forget to .... your books tomorrow!' the teacher said to the class.
3 Are you going to the kitchen? Can you .... me some water?
4 .... your camera with you when you go to Bangkok. It's beautiful there.
5 Are you going to the secretary's office? Can you .... these papers, please?
6 Shall I .... you a present from New York?

9.2 Fill the gaps with *take* or *bring back*.

1 Can I .... this book to read tonight? I'll .... it .... tomorrow.
2 When she went to Belgium, she .... me .... some chocolates.
3 Please .... my umbrella. You can .... it .... tomorrow.

9.3 Match the words on the left with the words on the right. Draw lines.

1 Yesterday he brought me   a these letters, please.
2 You must take   b bring your guitar.
3 Come to my house and   c some flowers.
4 Go to the secretary and take d food to the party.
5 Everybody is going to bring e your passport when you travel.

9.4 Fill the gaps with the correct form of *bring* or *take*.

1 She always .....*brings*...... me presents. Yesterday she .... me some chocolates.
2 Hello, I've .... you some flowers. I hope you like them!
3 I .... 72 photographs when I was in Rio de Janeiro.
4 She has .... my book, but she's going to .... it back tomorrow.

9.5 **Are you in your English lesson now? If *yes*, look at (a). If *no*, look at (b).**

(a) Name three things you always bring to the lesson.
(b) Name three things you always take to the lesson.

Name three things someone has brought you recently.

10 Get/got/got

A Get with adjectives: for changes

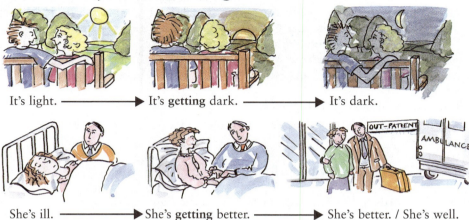

It's light. ⟶ It's **getting** dark. ⟶ It's dark.

She's ill. ⟶ She's **getting** better. ⟶ She's better. / She's well.

I'm **getting** tired. I want to go to bed.

It's raining! I'm **getting** wet!

B Get with nouns

If you don't have something you can **get** it.

I want to send a postcard. I have to **get** a stamp.
I've finished my studies. Now I want to **get** a job.
My friend is ill! Please **get** a doctor.
Do you want a drink? I can **get** some coffee.
I'm going to the shop to **get** a newspaper.
Where can I **get** a taxi?

C Get to (arrive at / reach a place)

How can I **get to** the airport? Take the airport bus at the bus station.
When you **get to** New York, ring me. OK, give me your number.

D Other phrases with get

Maria and David are **getting married** in April.
When you **get back** from Hong Kong,
   ring me. (= return / come home)
(See also **get up** in Unit 23.)

When I **get home**, I have my lunch.
I **get there** at 6 o'clock, so please
   ring me at 6.30.
[NOT get ~~to~~ home or get ~~to~~ there.]

Exercises

10.1 **Complete these sentences using (a), (b) or (c).**

1 I studied too much and I got (a) hot (b) tired (c) sick.
2 I ate too much and I got   (a) hot (b) tired (c) sick.
3 I sat in the sun too much and I got (a) hot (b) tired (c) sick.

10.2 **Complete these sentences using *get* and a word from the box.**

| better   light   dark   cold   wet |

1 The sun is going down. It *'s getting dark.*
2 When the sun comes up it ....
3 She's in hospital but she ....
4 It's raining! I ....!
5 Please close the window. I ....

10.3 **What/Who do you *get* if ...**

1 you want to post a letter? *a stamp*
2 somebody is ill?
3 you want a drink of water?
4 you want to write something down?
5 you want to read the news?
6 you want to go to the airport?
7 you want to earn some money?

10.4 **Fill the gaps in these sentences.**

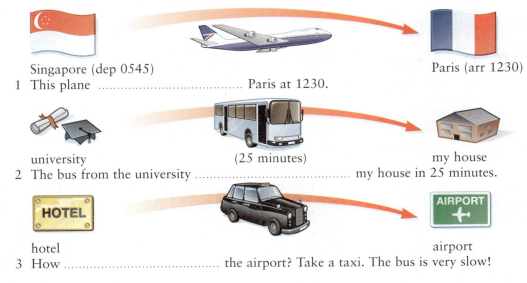

Singapore (dep 0545)   Paris (arr 1230)
1 This plane .... Paris at 1230.

university   (25 minutes)   my house
2 The bus from the university .... my house in 25 minutes.

hotel   airport
3 How .... the airport? Take a taxi. The bus is very slow!

10.5 **Answer the questions.**

1 In your country, how old are people when they get married?
2 When do people get married? Which day? Which month(s)?
3 What time do you get home every day? How do you get there?
4 Fill the gap: Now you can look at the key and .... the answers!

English Vocabulary in Use (elementary)   **25**

11 Phrasal verbs

A

A What are phrasal verbs?

Phrasal verbs have two parts: a verb + a preposition.

get up/on/over

I **got up** at 6.30 this morning. I'm tired now.
I hated my sister when I was young but now we **get on** very well.
He soon **got over** his cold. (= he got better quickly)

turn on/off/up/down

He always **turns on** the TV at 9 o'clock to watch the news.
It's a sunny day. **Turn** the light **off**.
Turn the TV **up**. I can't hear it.
Turn the TV **down**. It's too loud.

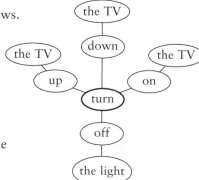

go on/off

Don't stop. **Go on** talking. It's very interesting.
A bomb **went off** in a London station today. Four people
   are still in hospital.

put something on

It's cold and windy outside. **Put** your coat **on**. *or* **Put on** your coat.

come on

Come on! We're late.

B One phrasal verb, different meanings

Note that one phrasal verb can often have different meanings.

turn down

She **turned down** the stereo. (= made it not so loud)
She **turned down** the invitation. (= refused it)

do up

She **did up** her coat.

She **did up** her flat.

take off

Our plane **takes off** at 12.30. (= leaves the ground)
She **took off** her shoes. (= removed them from her feet)

> **Tip:** Make a special page in your notebook. Write down any phrasal verbs you see or hear.

Exercises

11.1 Match a sentence on the left with a sentence on the right. Draw lines.

1 It's getting late.	a Turn it down then.
2 It's very cold today.	b Please turn your music down.
3 That funny programme is on soon.	c It's time to get up.
4 Her boyfriend left her.	d Do up your coat.
5 I'm trying to work.	e Put on your raincoat.
6 The flat is quite old.	f She got over it quickly.
7 It's raining today.	g Turn on the TV.
8 I don't want to accept that job.	h We can do it up nicely.

11.2 Put the correct prepositions in these sentences.

1 It's dark in here. Turn .... the lights.
2 Our plane takes .... at 6.25 and lands at 7.50.
3 Come ....! It's time to get ....
4 The children took .... their school uniforms when they got home.
5 It's time to turn .... the TV and go to bed now.
6 That teacher always gets .... her students.
7 The students went .... working until late at night.
8 When they got to the beach, he put .... his swimming trunks and ran down to the sea.

11.3 What is happening in these pictures? Use one of the phrasal verbs from the opposite page to describe each picture.

1 <u>They are doing up the hotel.</u>

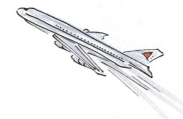

3 ....

2 ....

4 ....

11.4 Organise the words on the opposite page into groups, in any way that makes sense to you, for example, clothes, movement.

11.5 Replace the <u>underlined</u> words with a phrasal verb from the opposite page.

1 The plane <u>left</u> at midnight.
2 I <u>removed</u> my hat and coat.
3 She <u>continued</u> writing novels all her life.
4 He soon <u>got better from</u> the flu.

12 Everyday things

Things we do every day

I wake up

get up

go to the bathroom

have a shower

have breakfast /ˈbrekfəst/

listen to the radio /ˈlɪsən/

go to work

come home

make dinner

phone (*or* call) a friend

watch TV

go to bed

B **Sometimes I ...**

wash clothes /kləʊðz/

clean the house

go for a walk

write letters

C **Questions about everyday things**

How often do you read the newspaper / watch TV? Three times a week / every day, etc.
What time do you get up / go to work? Seven o'clock. / Half past eight. etc.
How do you go to work? By bus/train/car, etc.

D **Usually/normally (what I do typically)**

We say **I usually/normally** get up at eight o'clock, *but* today I got up at eight-thirty.
[NOT I used to / I'm used to get up at eight o'clock!]
(See also Units 3 and 6.)

Exercises

12.1 **Write the answers for *yourself*.**

1 I usually wake up at ....
2 I go to the bathroom and have ....
3 I usually have .... for breakfast.
4 I go to work by ....
5 I usually have a cup of tea/coffee at .... o'clock.

12.2 **What do they usually do?**

1 He ...listens to the radio every morning...............

2

She w.. (every Saturday)

3

He c.. (every weekend)

4

He w.. (every evening)

5

She g.. (every Sunday)

12.3 **Ask questions.**

	topic	question	answer
1	get up	What **time do you get up?**	Seven-thirty, usually.
2	go for a walk	How …	Every Saturday.
3	go to work	How …	By train.
4	have dinner	When …	Between seven and eight o'clock, usually.

13 Talking

A Say (say/said/said)

We use **say** when we report someone's words.
She **said** 'This is horrible!'
He **said that** he wanted a drink.

We use **say** when we ask about language.
A: **How do you say** 'book' in Spanish?
B: 'Libro'.

We **say hello / goodbye / please / thank you**
Happy Birthday / Merry Christmas / Happy New Year / Congratulations.
/kəngrætʃə`leɪʃnz/

B Tell (tell/told/told)

Tell is usually followed immediately by a person. **Say** is not followed immediately by a person.
He **told me** his name. [NOT He ~~said me~~ his name.]

We use **tell** when we want to know how to get to a place.
Can you tell me where the bus station is, please? [NOT Can you ~~say me~~ ...?]

We use **tell** with other **wh**-words too (**when, how, why, where**), e.g. you can **tell someone how** to do something, **where** something is, **why** something happened.

He **told me how** to send a fax. **Tell me when** you want to have dinner.
You can **tell someone the time / a story / a joke / your name / address / telephone number.**

C Ask

Ask is used for questions.
My sister **asked me** where I was going. (*or* My sister asked (me) 'Where are you going?')

A: Can I **ask you a question**?
B: Yes.
A: What day of the week were you born?
B: Thursday.

You can **ask someone the way / the time / a question.**

Ask somebody to do something and **ask someone for something.**
I **asked him to** turn off his radio. (*or* I said 'Please turn off your radio.')
She **asked for** the bill. (*or* She said 'Can I have the bill please?')

D Speak/talk/answer/reply

Do you **speak** Japanese?   [NOT Do you ~~talk~~ Japanese?]
I like **talking to** you. (having a conversation with you)
Can you **answer** the telephone / the door, please?
   (pick up the phone / open the door to see who it is)
I wrote a letter to him but he did not **reply.**
   (for letters/faxes/e-mails) (he did not send me a letter back).

Exercises

13.1 **Fill the gaps with the correct form of *say* or *tell*.**

1 Can you ...*tell*........ me where the Plaza Hotel is, please?
2 She .... me her name.
3 I .... goodbye to her.
4 'Please, ... me a story,' the little boy ....
5 'Come here!' the police officer ....
6 The teacher .... that the students were very good.

13.2 **What do you say?**

1 You want to know where the railway station is.
  Can ....?
2 You want to know the word for 'tree' in German.
  How ....?
3 You want to know the time.
  Excuse me, can you ....
  ....?

4 Your course is finished. You want to say goodbye to your teacher.
  I just want to ....
5 You want to know when the exam is.
  Can you ....?
6 The telephone rings. You are in the bathroom.
  (*To your friend*)
  Can you ....
  ....?

13.3 **Match the verbs on the left with the words on the right. Draw lines.**

1 Say	a	a letter
2 Answer	b	someone to help you
3 Ask for	c	Happy New Year
4 Reply to	d	the door
5 Tell	e	a friend
6 Talk to	f	someone a joke
7 Ask	g	the bill

13.4 **On the left are some things in different languages. Can you match them with the sentences on the right? Draw lines.**

1 La cuenta, por favor.	a	Say Merry Christmas in Swedish.
2 Berapa ini?	b	Say thank you in Arabic.
3 God jul!	c	Ask for the bill in Spanish.
4 Kon'nichi wa.	d	Ask how much something is in Malay.
5 Shukran.	e	Say good morning in Japanese.

14 Moving

A Without transport

walk   run   jump   dance   swim   jog   climb   fall

B Transport

You **go by** car / plane / bus / train / bike / motorbike / ship / taxi / underground [NOT by ~~a~~ car].

You **take a** bus / train / taxi / plane and you **take the** underground.

You **ride** a bicycle / bike / motorbike / horse.

You **drive** a car / bus / train.

The pilot **flies** a plane.

How did you get to Istanbul? We **flew** there.

If you **catch** the bus, train or plane, you arrive in time to get it.
If you **miss** the bus, train or plane, you arrive too late to get it.

You **arrive at** or **in** a place [NOT ~~to~~ a place]. The train arrived in Tokyo on time. The plane arrived late at Heathrow.

> **Tip:** When you are travelling you will probably see a lot of notices in English. Make a note of any new words and expressions you see.

See Unit 41 (Travelling) for more words about transport.

C Moving objects

'Please pass the salt.'

Can I help you carry your luggage?

Exercises

14.1 **Fill the gaps with verbs from A opposite. Write them in the correct form.**

1 Jack likes ....*jogging*............... round the park every morning but Betty prefers
....*walking*................ round it with her dog.
2 Everyone............................. at the party last night.
3 Every day Jane .... ten lengths of the swimming pool before breakfast.
4 James can .... very fast. He has won a lot of races.
5 Robert loves .... hills.
6 The old lady .... on her way home and broke her arm.
7 Sandra .... into the swimming pool and quickly .... to
the other side.
8 It is much better for you to .... to work than to go by car.

14.2 *Ride, drive, go by* or *take*? **Write the correct word(s) in the phrase.**

1 Can you .... a motorbike?
2 He works for a railway company. He .... a train.
3 She sometimes .... the underground to work.
4 He goes away from home a lot. He .... a lorry.
5 I prefer to .... a bus than .... car.
6 Would you like to .... an elephant.
7 You never forget how to .... a bicycle.
8 I usually .... a taxi when it rains.

14.3 **Answer these questions. Use** *every day, once a week, once a year* **or** *never.*

1 How often do you walk to work or school? *I walk to work every day.*
2 Have you got a bike? How often do you ride it?
3 How often do you go swimming? Do you go in the sea or in a swimming pool?
4 How often do you go jogging?
5 How often do you drive a car?
6 How often do you go dancing?
7 Do you often go climbing?

14.4 **What other things do we often ask people to pass at the dinner table?**

Write down *Please pass* + a noun six times. *Please pass the sugar.*

14.5 **Put these sentences into the past tense with the word** *yesterday.*

1 Jim runs a mile every day. *He ran a mile yesterday.*
2 Maria often drives her grandmother to the city.
3 Bill catches the 9.45 train to London every day.
4 I sometimes take a taxi home from the station.
5 Jane often falls when she rides her bike.

15 Conjunctions and connecting words

A Basic conjunctions

Conjunctions join two parts of a sentence and help to show the connection between the two parts of the sentence.

conjunction	function	example
and	tells you more	We went home and went straight to bed.
but	makes a contrast	They are rich but they aren't happy.
because	answers the question *why*?	We went home because we were tired.
so	tells you the result	We went home early, so we missed the end of the concert.
when	answers the question *when*?	We went home when Jane wanted to.
before, after	answers the question *what happened first*?	We went home before the concert ended. We went home after Max Jones had sung his first song.
although, though /ðəʊ/	tells you something surprising	We went home although / though we did not really want to.
if	makes a condition	We will go home if we are tired.

B Other connecting words

The words in this table are useful for making connections between words and phrases.

word	function	example
only	says something is not very big or not very much	He sleeps only 3 hours every night.
even	says something is surprising or unusual	Even their 10-year-old son works in the shop.
like	makes a comparison	She looks like her dad.
than	used after a comparative adjective or adverb	She works harder than he does.
also, too, as well	says something is extra	He works in the shop and she does also / too / as well.

Exercises

15.1 Choose one of the underlined words to complete the sentence.

1 Sam liked school because/although/if he had many friends there.
2 Sam left school so/but/and he joined the navy.
3 He hadn't travelled much but/before/after he joined the navy.
4 Sam was seasick when/if/so he left the navy.
5 He got a job in a bank because/although/and he had no qualifications.
6 He will stay at the bank when/if/though he likes it there.

15.2 Write down ten sentences from the table. Use each of the conjunctions once.

	after	she loves him.
	although	she doesn't love him.
Mary agreed to marry Paul	and	she loved him.
	because	she didn't love him.
	before	they had two sons.
	but	he moves to London.
	if	he moved to London.
Mary will marry Paul	so	he was a pop star.
	though	they decided to set up a business together.
	when	

15.3 Write each of the conjunctions in A in your own language.

15.4 Fill in the gaps with words from the table in B.

I love swimming and my brother loves swimming (1)... . Almost all my family loves swimming. (2).. my grandmother swims every day. She swims (3).............................. a fish. (4).. my father doesn't like it very much. I can swim better (5).. my father.

15.5 Think about your family and your habits. Write sentences using *only, even, than, like, also, too* and *as well* about your habits.

I play tennis and my mother plays as well. My mother plays better than I do.

15.6 Complete these sentences for *yourself*.

1 I am learning English because ....
2 I'll learn more English if ....
3 I am learning English and ....
4 I am learning English although ....
5 I started learning English when ....
6 I can speak some English, so ....
7 I'll learn more English but ....

16 Time words (1): days, months and seasons

A Basic time words

There are:
365 days in a year
12 months   /mʌnθs/   in a year
52 weeks in a year
7 days in a week
2 weeks in a fortnight
24 hours in a day
60 minutes in an hour. (We say **an** hour /ˈaʊə/)
60 seconds in a minute
100 years in a century

B Days of the week

Sunday /ˈsʌndeɪ/, Monday /ˈmʌndeɪ/, Tuesday, Wednesday /ˈwenzdeɪ/, Thursday, Friday, Saturday.

The names of the days always begin with a capital letter in English.

Saturday + Sunday = the weekend

the day before ← yesterday ← today → tomorrow → the day after
yesterday   tomorrow

Monday (before 12 a.m.) = Monday morning
Monday (between 12 a.m. and 6 p.m.) = Monday afternoon
Monday (after 6 p.m.) = Monday evening
We say **on** + days of the week: on Monday, on Saturday, etc. I saw her **on Friday**, **on Tuesday** evening.
We say **at** + the weekend: I went to the cinema **at the weekend**.

C Months and seasons

Months: January, February, March, April, May, June, July, August, September, October, November, December.
The names of the months always begin with a capital letter in English.

Some countries have four seasons: spring, summer, autumn /ˈɔːtəm/ and winter.

We say in + months/seasons: in July, in December, in (the) spring, in (the) summer, etc.
My birthday is **in July**. [NOT ~~on~~ July] Birds sing **in (the) spring**.

> **Tip:** Write the day and date in English when you do an English exercise.

Exercises

16.1 Complete the sentences with a word from A opposite.

1 There are 3,600 seconds in ....
2 There are 1,200 months in ....
3 There are 168 hours in ....
4 There are 8,760 hours in ....

16.2 Recite (a) the days of the week and (b) the months of the year.

16.3 Complete this British children's song about the number of days in each month.

Thirty days has S........................... ,
A..........................., J........................... and N........................... .
All the rest have .... ,
Except for F........................... dear
Which has twenty eight days clear
And .... in each **leap year** (= every four years).

16.4 These abbreviations are often used for the days of the week and the months. Write the names out in full.

1 Mon.   5 Wed.   9 Feb.
2 Aug.   6 Jan.   10 Sept.
3 Oct.   7 Apr.   11 Tues.
4 Sat.   8 Th.   12 Nov.

16.5 What are the next few letters in each case? Explain why.

1 S   M   T   W   ?   ?   ?
2 J   F   M   A   M   J   J   ?   ?   ?   ?   ?
3 S   S   ?   ?

16.6 There are six mistakes in this paragraph. Correct the mistakes.

I'm going to a party on saturday for Jill's birthday. Her birthday is on thursday but she wanted to have the party on a Weekend. She's having a barbecue. I think june is a good month to have a birthday because of the weather. I love going to barbecues on the summer. My birthday is in Winter and it's too cold to eat outside!

16.7 Quiz: How quickly can you answer these questions?

1 How many seconds in quarter of an hour?
2 What is the third day of the week?
3 What month is your birthday in?
4 What day will it be the day after tomorrow?
5 What day was it the day before yesterday?
6 How many minutes are there in half an hour?
7 What day is it today?
8 What day will it be tomorrow?
9 What is the seventh month?
10 What day was it yesterday?
11 What century is it?
12 What month is it?

17 Time words (2)

Time in relation to NOW

Now means at this moment. **Then** means at another moment (usually in the past).

It is 10 **o'clock** now.
I got up **2 hours ago, at** 8 o'clock.
An hour ago it was 9 o'clock.

two years   **for two years**
1994   1996   **from 1994 to 1996**   *1994 ⟶ 1996*
               from 2010 to 2012

last year / last week / last Saturday
next year / next week / next summer

It is July **now**.
Last month it was June.
Next month it will be August.

When we talk about time in general, we talk about **the past, the present** and **the future**. We talk about the past, the present and the future forms of the verb, for example

In the past people didn't have television.
People may travel to Mars **in the future**.

I'll be with you **in a moment**. (= a very short time)
Jane's in Paris **at the moment**. (= now)

See you **soon**! (= in a short time)

We met **recently**. (= not long ago)

Frequency adverbs

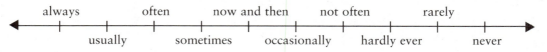

It **always** snows in Russia in winter.
It **often** rains in Britain.
The temperature in London **hardly ever** gets to 35°. (= almost never)
The Ancient Romans **never** went to America or Australia.

Notice the use of **a** in these expressions of frequency.
once (= one time) a week: I go swimming **once** a week, every Saturday.
twice (= two times) a day: I clean my teeth **twice a day**.
three times a year: I see my uncle **three times a year**.
four times a month: I play football **four or five times a month**.

Exercises

17.1 Fill the gaps with a preposition from A opposite.

⁽¹⁾........ the past, Rosa worked in many different countries. Rosa worked in Hong Kong ⁽²⁾........ three years, ⁽³⁾........ 1993 ⁽⁴⁾........ 1996. ⁽⁵⁾........ the moment she is working in Tokyo. She will stay there ⁽⁶⁾........ two more years.

17.2 Draw lines to match the centuries to their time.

1 the 19th century
2 the 22nd century
3 the 18th century   the past
4 the 21st century   the present
5 the 20th century   the future

17.3 Read the sentences and answer the questions.

1 Peter will get his exam results very soon.
Do you think Peter will get them next year, next month or tomorrow?
2 Harriet and Rupert met for the first time recently.
Do you think they first met last year, six months ago or a week ago?
3 I'll help you in a moment.
Do you think I'll help you next week, in two hours or in a few minutes?

17.4 Are these sentences true about *you*? If not, write them out correctly. Use other frequency adverbs from B on the opposite page.

1 I always go swimming on Fridays. *I sometimes go swimming on Fridays. I often go swimming on Saturdays.*
2 I normally go to school/work by bus.   6 I often wear a hat.
3 I hardly ever play football.   7 I rarely eat chocolate.
4 I occasionally watch TV.   8 I always go to bed at 10.
5 I rarely drink milk.   9 I never go to the theatre.

17.5 Look at the table and make sentences using expressions like *once a week, three times a month*, etc.

	play tennis	*practise the piano*	*have a business meeting in Germany*
John	Mondays and Thursdays	Saturdays	the first Friday every month
Sally and Amy	Tuesdays, Fridays and Saturdays	every morning and every evening	once in January, March, May, July, August and December every year.

17.6 Write a paragraph about your own life using as many as possible of the words and expressions from the opposite page.

18 Places

A General place words

Come **here** please. (to me, to where I am)
Do you know Lima? I'm going **there** in April. (not here, another place)
I'm coming **back** from Portugal in May. (to here again, to this place)
There are books and papers **everywhere** in my room. (in all parts / all places)
(See unit 7.)

B Positions

The **top** of the mountain.

The **middle** of the road.

The **bottom** of the glass.

The **front** of the car.

The **side** of the car.

The **back** of the car.

The **beginning** of the motorway.
The **end** of the motorway.

C Left and right

This is his **left** hand.

This is his **right** hand.

In York Street, there is a cinema **on the left** and a restaurant **on the right**.

D Home and away

Is Mary **at home**? (in her house / flat)
No, sorry, she's **out.** (at the shops / at work / at school)
No, sorry, she's **away.** (in another town / city or country)
No, sorry, she's **abroad.** (in another country)

Exercises

18.1 Fill the gaps with *here* or *there*.

1 Please bring it .... (See Unit 9 for **bring.**)
2 Are you coming .... next week? (See Unit 7 for **come.**)
3 This letter is for a teacher at the university. Can you take it .... ? (See Unit 8 for **take.**)
4 I want to leave this letter in Nora's office. Are you going .... ?

18.2 Complete the sentences.

HOME   PARIS

23 October

6 November

Key
Restaurants ●

1 What is Mary doing on 6 November?   2 Is there just one restaurant in Scoffton?
She's coming ....   No, there are restaurants ....

18.3 Mark the positions on the tree and on the bus.

1 The top of the tree.
2 The middle of the tree.
3 The bottom of the tree.
4 The front of the bus.
5 The side of the bus.
6 The back of the bus.

18.4 Answer these questions about *yourself* and about this book.

1 Are you studying English at home or abroad?
2 Are you going away this year?
3 What have you got in your left or right hand at the moment?
4 What is there at the end of this book?
5 Where is the unit on **Have** in this book? (beginning/middle/end?)
6 Where is the Unit on **Feelings**? (beginning/middle/end?)

18.5 Fill the gap with *out*, *away* or *abroad*.

1 I'd like to work .... and learn about a new country.
2 Is Lily here? No, she's .... but she'll be back in about five minutes.
3 I'm going .... tomorrow to my sister's. She lives about 50 miles north of here.
4 When we go .... we like to go .... and see new countries.

19 Manner

Manner = **how** we do something

A Fast and slow

This car goes very **fast**. It's a **fast** car.　　This car goes very **slowly**. It's a **slow** car.

B Right and wrong

This sentence is **right**.　　I like coffee very much.　　✓
This sentence is **wrong**.　　I like very much coffee.　　✗

C Loud and quiet /laʊd/ and /ˈkwaɪət/

The music is too **loud**.　　　　　　　　It's very **quiet** here.

The teacher speaks very **quietly**. We can't hear him.
She sang loudly.

D Well and badly

She's a **good** driver. She drives **well**.
He's a **bad** driver. He drives **badly**.

E Way

Way means **how** someone does something.

He's speaking **in a friendly way**.　She's speaking **in an unfriendly way**.

Exercises

19.1 **Complete the sentences.**

1 This train is **slow**. It goes very ...<u>slowly</u>......
2 He is a **bad** singer. He sings very ....
3 She is always **loud**. She speaks very ....
4 He's a **fast** swimmer. He swims very ....
5 This girl is **quiet**. She always speaks ....
6 He's a **good** English-speaker. He speaks English ....

19.2 **Which do you think is better? Use your dictionary if you want to.**

1 A loud person or a quiet person?
2 A fast bus or a slow bus?
3 A friendly person or an unfriendly person?
4 A right answer or a wrong answer?
5 To speak politely or impolitely?
6 To speak in a strange way or in a normal way?

19.3 **Find words from the left-hand page.**

```
w   r   o   n   g   o
e   c   i  (b   a   d)
l   u   b   g   e   z
l   o   u   d   h   i
s   e   f   a   s   t
```

19.4 **Use a dictionary. Are the definitions right or wrong?**

word	definition	right (✔)	wrong (✘)
suddenly	very slowly		✘
sadly	in an unhappy way		
strangely	not in a normal way		
quickly	very slowly		
easily	with no difficulty		

19.5 **Make sentences about yourself and your friends/family. Use the new words opposite.**

I play tennis well.

20 Irregular verbs

Most verbs in English are regular but some of the most common verbs in English are irregular. The forms here are the infinitive (go, come), the past simple (went, came) and the past participle (gone, come).

A All forms the same

cost cost cost	cut /kʌt/ cut cut	hurt hurt hurt
let let let	put /pʊt/ put put	shut /ʃʌt/ shut shut

B Two different forms

run ran run	read /riːd/ read /red/ read /red/	feel felt felt
keep kept kept	sleep slept slept	leave left left
come came come	become became become	
bring brought brought	buy bought bought	catch caught caught
fight fought fought	teach taught taught	think thought thought
find found found	spend spent spent	learn learnt learnt
pay paid /peɪd/ paid	say said /sed/ said	
win won won	lose lost lost	shine shone shone
sell sold sold	tell told told	sit sat sat
meet met met	get got got	shoot shot shot
stand stood stood	understand understood understood	
make made made	have had had	do did done
hear heard heard	beat beat beaten	

C Three different forms

be was/were been	go went gone	begin began begun
drink drank drunk	sing sang sung	swim swam swum
fly flew flown	know knew known	throw threw thrown
break broke broken	choose chose chosen	speak spoke spoken
steal stole stolen	wake woke woken	take took taken
wear wore worn	drive drove driven	ride rode ridden
rise rose risen	write wrote written	eat ate eaten
give gave given	forget forgot forgotten	fall fell fallen

Tip: When you learn a new irregular verb, add it to one of the groups of verbs on this page.

Exercises

20.1 Do you know what the verbs opposite mean? Write out the infinitive form of each of the verbs with its meaning in your own language beside it. Use a dictionary if you want to.

20.2 Write these words out in their three forms. Then find a verb on the opposite page which has the opposite meaning. Write it out in its three forms.

1 open *open, opened, opened; shut, shut, shut*
2 give   5 walk   8 rise
3 come   6 wake   9 win
4 make   7 remember   10 buy

20.3 Use the pictures and complete this story about Jane yesterday.

Yesterday Jane .(1)................ up at 7.00. She .(2)................ an apple and she .(3)................ a cup of hot chocolate. Then she got in her car and .(4)................ to work. At work she .(5)................ a newspaper and then she .(6)................ some letters. At lunch-time she .(7)................ in the park for half an hour and then she .(8)................ a sandwich. After lunch she .(9)................ at her desk again and .(10)................ some telephone calls. In the evening she .(11)................ the office at six o'clock and .(12)................ some Japanese visitors. They .(13)................ to a restaurant together. After a busy day Jane .(14)................ very well.

20.4 Choose the best verbs opposite. Complete the sentences with the correct past participle form.

1 We have .... in the sea every day this week.
2 Where is my bike? Someone has .... it!
3 I have .... a long time on this work.
4 That boy has .... very lazy recently.
5 I hope Jack has .... the bus and won't be late home.
6 Poor John. He has .... his leg badly. But he hasn't .... it.

20.5 Write sentences of your own with verbs from the box. Use the past tense.

> bring   choose   fall   feel   fly   keep
> pay   speak   teach   tell   think   win

20.6 Read all three parts of all the verbs on the opposite page aloud. Then cover parts two and three. Can you remember what they are?

21 Common uncountable words

A What is countable?

apples   shoes   plates   COUNTABLE (You can count them: 4 apples, 2 shoes)

sugar   money   luggage   UNCOUNTABLE (You can't count it: NOT 3 ~~luggages~~)

Can I have **three apples** and **some sugar**, please?
Are these **shoes** yours? **Is** this **luggage** yours?

B Everyday uncountable words

This **furniture** is modern.

The **traffic** is bad today.

I'll give you some **advice** about your future.

He can give you some useful **information** about Bangkok.

There is some bad **news** today.

It's terrible **weather** today.

Accommodation here is expensive.

I need some fresh **air**.

Studying is **hard work**.

Air **travel** is faster than rail **travel**.

C Food

A lot of uncountable nouns are kinds of food and drink.

rice   spaghetti   butter   bread   milk   water   tea   coffee

Note: When we want to say how much we want, we say, three loaves of bread, two litres of milk, a kilo of apples.

Tip: When you learn a new noun, write it down in a phrase which shows if it is countable or uncountable.

Exercises

21.1 Fill the gaps with an uncountable noun opposite.

1 I'd like to buy a car but I haven't got enough ....
2 Cows give us .... and ....
3 If you don't know what to do, ask your parents for some ....
4 The .... at the seaside is very good for you.
5 Rob left school last month and is now looking for ....
6 There is always a lot of .... in central London.

21.2 Match the words on the right with the words on the left.

1	heavy	information
2	useful	travel
3	bad	water
4	modern	luggage
5	brown	news
6	cold	furniture
7	space	bread

21.3 Find an adjective to go with the uncountable nouns in the box.

cold weather, British money

> weather money sugar traffic advice accommodation air
> work rice spaghetti butter milk tea coffee

21.4 Fill the gaps with the correct form of the verb *be*.

1 Accommodation in the city centre .... expensive.
2 Spaghetti with Italian tomato sauce .... very good.
3 The weather in Scotland .... best in the autumn.
4 The news .... better today than it .... yesterday.
5 Work .... the most important thing in Sam's life.
6 Their furniture .... very old and very beautiful.

21.5 Correct the mistakes in these sentences.

1 The news ~~are~~ not very good today.
   The news is not very good today.
2 Where can I get some informations about your country?
3 Let me give you an advice.
4 Cook these spaghetti for ten minutes.
5 Can I have a bread, please?
6 Mary is looking for a new work.
7 We should buy some new furnitures.
8 The east of the country usually has a better weather than the west.
9 We went on two long travels last year.
10 I must find a new accommodation soon.

22 Common adjectives: good and bad things

A (+) 'good' adjectives

A **good** restaurant.    A **better** restaurant.    The **best** restaurant in town.

This restaurant is **better than** that one.
nice (+) **lovely** (++) **wonderful** (+++) **excellent** (++++)

A: That's a **nice** jacket.
B: Thank you.

A: It's a **lovely** day today!
B: Yes, it is.

A **wonderful** view /ˈwʌndəfəl/

Mary's a **wonderful** person.
Everybody loves her.

A: Do you want to go to London on Saturday?
B: That's an **excellent** (= very good) idea!

When you answer and want to say how you feel:
A: The train arrives at six o'clock; dinner is at seven.
B: **Excellent! / Great! / Wonderful! / Lovely! / Perfect!**

B (-) 'bad' adjectives

bad (**worse** / **the worst**) (-)   **awful** (- -)   **terrible** (- - -)   **horrible** (- - -)

bad weather

My hair is **awful!**

The weather last year was **worse than** this year. /wɜːs/
Tim is a **horrible** person. Nobody likes him. (used about people)
I had a **terrible** day at work today. (used about situations)
The traffic's **terrible** at 5 o'clock on Fridays.

Note: We often say **not bad** when we are speaking:
A: I get $500 a week in my job.
B: That's **not bad!** (= good!)

You can say these adjectives with **how**:
A: I have to get up at 5.30 tomorrow.
B: Oh, **how awful! / horrible!** [NOT ~~how bad~~]

Exercises

22.1 Fill the gaps, as in the example.

1 My hair's ...*awful*... I must go to the hairdresser's.
2 The weather's .... I don't want to go out.
3 The traffic is .... in the city centre. Take the train.
4 That's a(n) .... idea! Let's do it!
5 How ....! Three exams on the same day!
6 What a .... house! The sea is only 100 metres away!
7 My timetable's not .... I'm free on Wednesdays and Fridays.

22.2 What can you say?   Someone says to you …

1 Do you like my new jacket?
2 I have to get up at 4.30 tomorrow morning.
3 Shall we go out for dinner tonight?
4 (*In your town*) Excuse me. Is there a good restaurant in this town?
5 What sort of person is your English teacher?

22.3 What goes together? Match a description from the left with an expression from the right. Draw lines.

1 Blue sky, sun 25°.   a Wonderful news.
2 5 stars (★★★★★), very famous.   b Awful weather.
3 Bad person. Nobody likes him/her.   c Lovely weather.
4 90 out of 100 in an exam.   d An excellent idea.
5 Grey sky, wind, rain, 11°.   e The best hotel in town.
6 We can take a taxi.   f A horrible person.

22.4 Use a dictionary. Put these new words into the *good* or *bad* column.

dreadful   ghastly   gorgeous   marvellous   horrendous   fine   superb   brilliant

good (+)	bad (-)
	dreadful

22.5 Look at the adjectives in 22.4. Think of two nouns to go with each of the adjectives.
dreadful weather/film

23 Common adjectives: people

In this unit, ** = normal, **** = stronger

A Saying positive (+)/good things about people

Nice is the most common word used for people who we like / who are good.
Mary's very **nice**.
Richard's a **nice** man.

If we want to make **nice** stronger, we can use **wonderful**.
nice (**) ——————➤ wonderful (****)

Ron is a **wonderful** teacher. All the students love him.
But we don't say 'Mary is ~~very~~ wonderful', we just say 'Mary is wonderful'.

If someone is good to other people, we use **kind**.
She's very **kind**; she helps me with the children.

Other 'good' things about people

My teacher is a **lovely** man. (= very kind / I like him very much) /ˈlʌvlɪ/
My friend Neil is very **easy-going**. (= relaxed, easy to be with)
Maureen's a **happy** person. (≠ **an unhappy** person)
All my friends are more **intelligent** than me. (= clever, good at school subjects, etc.)

B Saying negative (-)/bad things about people

Marcia is **not very nice**.

not very nice (**) ——————➤ horrible (****)

Margaret is a **horrible** woman; nobody likes her.
My uncle is a **difficult** person. He is never happy.
That waiter is **stupid**. I asked for coffee and he has given me tea! (**stupid** **** is a very
   strong word)
I don't like **selfish** people. (= people who think only of themselves)

C Little children

We often say that little children are **good** or **well-behaved**. If they are not, we say they are
naughty.
Tim is very **good / well-behaved**, but his little sister is very **naughty**.

D Prepositions

Jean was nice/kind/wonderful **to** me when I was in hospital.
You were horrible **to** me yesterday!
It was nice/kind **of** you to remember my birthday.

Exercises

23.1 **What do you think B said? Complete the sentences.**

1 A: Mary's very nice.
   B: She's more than nice, she's ....

2 A: Was George not very nice to you?
   B: He was really ....!

3 A: Let me carry your bag.
   B: Thanks, that's ....

4 A: Is your little brother well-behaved?
   B: No, he's ....

23.2 **Complete the word puzzle. Use the letters of *selfish* and words from the opposite page.**

	2 w						
	o						
	n		4 d		6 e		
	d			5			
1 s	e	3 l	f	i	s	7 h	
	r						
u	f			e	-	r	
	v	e			g		
	l		u				
		y			b		
			t				

23.3 **Circle the words that describe *you*.**

> **I am:** easy-going   sometimes difficult   kind to animals   sometimes stupid
> happy   intelligent   selfish   horrible to some people   nice to my friends

23.4 **Fill in the correct prepositions.**

1 The teacher is never horrible ..*to*.. the students.
2 It is kind .... you to help me.
3 Barbara was wonderful .... me when I needed a friend.
4 It was nice .... her to ring me.

24 Words and prepositions

A Verbs

Some verbs are usually followed by a preposition.
I **listen to** the radio in bed in the morning.
I **waited for** the bus for half an hour yesterday.
I **asked for** a black coffee, not a white one.
Where do I **pay for** our meal?
This book **belongs to** Sarah Smith.

What are you **thinking about**?
Helena **thanked** her mother **for** the present.
Jamie **apologised for** being late.

I'm sorry.

B Same verb, different preposition

Some verbs have different meanings when they are used
with different prepositions, for example, **look**.

children — after — look — at — a book
a key — for — look
forward to
a party

I love **looking at** old photographs.
If you want to find something, for example, your key, you must **look for** it.
Parents **look after** their children (= they take care of them).
You **look forward to** something nice in the future, for example, a friend's letter, a holiday.

C Adjectives

Some adjectives are also followed by prepositions.
I'm **good at** geography but **bad at** maths.
I'm **interested in** (hearing) all your news.
He is **afraid of** mice.
John is **proud of** winning a medal and his mother is **proud of** him.

Note: You are **used to** (*or* **accustomed to**) what you know well; you have to **get used to** /
accustomed to something new, for example a new school or driving on the other side of
the road; you are used to doing something, I'm used to getting up early, I always do.

D Grammar

Prepositions are followed by a noun: Joe is **good at tennis** *or*
the -ing form of the verb: Joe is **good at playing** the piano [NOT good at ~~play~~ the piano].

Tip: Look carefully at prepositions when you read in English. Make a note of any
phrases which use prepositions in a new way.

Exercises

24.1 **Match a phrase on the left with a phrase on the right, to make seven sentences.**

1 John is waiting	for his mistake.
2 This bicycle belongs	about the holidays.
3 The children thanked their grandmother	for a train to London.
4 Sally is listening	to the hotel.
5 He apologised	for our tickets.
6 Let me pay	to her walkman.
7 Billy is thinking	for the money.

24.2 **Complete these sentences with a preposition and an appropriate noun or pronoun.**

1 Joanna can't read yet but she likes looking ......*at books.*......
2 A nurse looks ....
3 I can't find my glasses? Could you help me look ....?
4 It's my birthday soon. I'm really looking ....
5 Why are you looking .... in that way? Is my face dirty?
6 I don't like my job very much. I'm looking ....
7 Alex is going to France in July. He is looking ....
8 I often look .... when their parents go out.

24.3 **Fill the gaps with a preposition.**

Anne has got used [(1)]........ her new job and is doing well there. She is very good [(2)]........ talking to customers. She always listens [(3)]........ them. She is very interested [(4)]........ sport and she belongs [(5)]........ a tennis club and a swimming club. Her parents were very proud [(6)]........ her when she won a medal for swimming last year.

24.4 **Hiroshi is a visitor from Japan. Make sentences about what he found strange, at first, in Britain.**

1 driving on the left ✓ *Hiroshi was used to driving on the left.*
2 speaking English every day ✗ *He wasn't used to speaking English every day.*
3 eating British food ✗
4 traffic jams ✓
5 expensive shops ✓
6 British money ✗

24.5 **Answer these questions about *yourself*.**

1 What were you good at at school? What were you bad at?
2 What do you usually ask for when you go to a café?
3 What are you proud of?
4 What are you afraid of?
5 What kind of music do you like listening to?
6 What are you looking forward to?
7 Do you belong to any clubs?
8 Are you used to eating different kinds of food?

25 Prefixes

Prefixes (at the beginning of words) can help you to understand what a new word means. Here are some common prefixes.

prefix	meaning	examples
ex (+noun)	was but not now	ex-wife, ex-president
half (+noun or adjective)	50% of something	half-price, half-hour
in, im (+adjective)	not	informal, impossible
non (+adjective or noun)	not	non-smoking
pre	before	pre-school
re (+verb)	again	redo, rewrite
un (+adjective or noun)	not	unhappy, unsafe

An **ex-wife** is a wife who is now divorced.
President Gorbachev is an **ex-President** of Russia.
A **half-hour** journey is a journey of 30 minutes.
Something that cost £10 yesterday and costs £5 today is **half-price**.
Informal clothes are clothes like jeans and trainers. Formal clothes are things like a suit.
If something is **impossible**, you can't do it. It is impossible to read with your eyes closed.
A **non-smoking** room is a room where people may not smoke.
Pre-school children are children who are still too young to go to school.
To **redo** something is to do it a second time and to **rewrite** something is to write it a second time.
Unhappy means sad, the opposite of happy.
Unsafe means dangerous, the opposite of safe.

THIS BRIDGE IS UNSAFE!

Tip: Sometimes words with prefixes have a hyphen (-), e.g. a half-hour programme, and sometimes they don't, e.g. an impossible question. Use a dictionary when you are not sure if there is a hyphen or not.

Exercises

25.1   Choose one of the words from the prefix table to fit in these sentences.

1 This part of the restaurant is ...non-smoking....
2 I can't read this. Please .... your homework.
3 In .... English we often say 'Hi'.
4 I liked school but my sister was very .... there.
5 I bought two T-shirts because they were .... in the sale.
6 Don't walk on that wall – the notice says it is ....

25.2   Write your own sentences to show what these words mean.

ex-wife   ex-president   redo
impossible   pre-school

25.3   What do you think these words and phrases mean? Look at the table on the opposite page to help you.

1 an ex-husband *a husband who is now divorced from his wife*
2 pre-exam nerves
3 an incorrect answer
4 an unread book
5 to retell a story
6 a half-brother
7 an unfinished letter
8 a non-alcoholic drink
9 to reread a book
10 to readdress a letter

25.4   Find one more example of a word using the prefixes in the table. Use a dictionary to help you. Write a phrase or sentence using your word.

ex: *My ex-boss lives near me.*
half: *You stop at half-time in a football match.*

25.5   Write a paragraph with at least eight of the example words from the table.

25.6   Find the negative forms of these words. Use a dictionary if necessary.

1 possible *impossible*
2 comfortable
3 safe
4 formal
5 smoking
6 happy
7 polite
8 correct

26 Suffixes

Suffixes come at the end of words. They help you to understand the meaning of a new word. Here are some common suffixes.

suffix	meaning	examples
er, or (noun)	person	worker, swimmer, instructor
er, or (noun)	machine, thing	cooker, word processor
ful (adjective)	full of	useful, beautiful
ology (noun)	subject of study	sociology, psychology
ics (noun, singular)	subject of study	economics, politics
less (adjective)	without	useless, endless
ly	makes an adverb from an adjective	sadly, happily
ness	makes an abstract noun from an adjective	happiness, sadness
y	makes an adjective from a noun	sandy, sunny

He's a hard **worker**. He works 12 hours a day.
Her tennis is much better now that she has a new **instructor**.
She's a very good **swimmer**.
She was in the Olympic team.
We've got a new gas **cooker**
   so the food should be delicious!

Thanks for the information. It was very **useful**.
What a **beautiful** photo. I think it will win the competition.

Studying **sociology** teaches you about society.
Studying **psychology** teaches you about people.

Economics is the study of money and finance.
Although he is a very good Member of Parliament, he has never studied **politics**.

This book is no help at all – it's **useless**.
I can't finish this book – it's **endless**.

He was late for work so he went **quickly** to the station.
The little child danced **happily** across the grass.

The mother was smiling with **happiness** as she held her baby in her arms.
They said goodbye with great **sadness** because they
   knew they would probably never meet again.

That beach is very popular with tourists
   because it is long and **sandy**.
It's a lovely **sunny** day – let's go to the beach.

Exercises

26.1 Which of the example words do these pictures illustrate?

1 a s*unny day*........................ 3 a golf i............................ 5 a s..

2 He's smiling h................ 4 a w............................ 6 a u............................ thing

26.2 Match the adjectives with the nouns in the box. Some adjectives go with more than one noun.

electric cooker / guitar

1 electric   3 beautiful   5 sunny   7 useful   9 useless
2 fast   4 sandy   6 hard   8 endless

| worker cooker beach weather car idea |
| book swimmer guitar smile picture fun |

26.3 Match these books with their subjects – *sociology, psychology, economics* or *politics*.

1 The Role of the President in the US Congress
2 British Society in the 1950s
3 Banking Today
4 Why People Smile

26.4 Are there suffixes in your language? Write a translation or an explanation for the suffixes in the table.

26.5 What do you think these words and phrases mean? Use the information about prefixes and suffixes in the table to help you.

1 zoology *the study of animals*   6 painless
2 a traveller   7 badly
3 slowly   8 a tin opener
4 hopeful   9 mathematics
5 rainy   10 a footballer

27 Words you may confuse

This unit looks at words which are easy to mix up.

A Similar sounds

quite/quiet
This book is **quite** good. /ˈkwaɪt/  bad ——→ quite good ——→ good
My bedroom is very **quiet**. /ˈkwaɪət/ = silent / no noise

lose/loose
A: Why do I always **lose** my keys! /luːz/
B: Here they are.
A: Oh, thank you!

If you **lose** something, you do not
know where it is / you can't find it.

These trousers are very **loose**. /ˈluːs/ (loose means they are not tight,
because they are too big)

fell/felt
Fell is from **fall/fell/fallen.**
Yesterday I **fell** and broke my arm.
Felt is from **feel/felt/felt.**
I **felt** ill yesterday, but I **feel**
OK today.

cooker/cook
This **cooker** costs £500. (= the thing you cook on)
He is a very good **cook**. (= the person who cooks)

B Similar or related meanings

Do you want to borrow it?

lend/borrow
If you **lend** something, you *give* it.
If you **borrow** something, you *get* it.
Sam wants a bicycle:
SAM: Will you **lend** me your bicycle? (= you *give* it to me for one day/an hour, etc.)
or Can I **borrow** your bicycle? (= I *get* it
RITA: Yes, take it.
SAM: Thanks.

check/control
The passport officer **checked** my passport. (= looked at it)
The mouse **controls** the computer. (= tells it what to do)

C Other words often mixed up

In English the **afternoon** is from about 12 o'clock till 5 or 6 p.m.
The **evening** is from 5 or 6 p.m. until about 9 or 10 p.m.
After 9 or 10 p.m. it is the **night**.
They're **waiting for** the bus.
I **hope** I pass my exams. (= I really want to pass)
I have not studied; I **expect** I'll fail my exams. (= it's probable)

Exercises

27.1 Fill the gaps with words from A opposite. The first letter is given.

1 Please be ..*quiet*.. The baby is sleeping.
2 If you l..................... your passport you must call the Embassy.
3 I f..................... tired this morning, but I am OK now.
4 We are going to buy a c..................... for our new kitchen.
5 She f..................... and broke her leg. She had to go to hospital.
6 It's q..................... cold today.
7 These shoes are very l..................... I need smaller ones.
8 My sister is a good c..................... I love eating at her house.

27.2 Put a tick in the right box for each word. Look at the example.

word	sounds like?	yes (✔)	sounds like?	yes (✔)
lose	juice		shoes	✔
loose	juice		shoes	
quite	right		**higher**	
quiet	right		**higher**	

27.3 Answer these questions.

1 What does a mouse do to a computer? It ....*controls it.*....
2 What does the passport officer do to your passport? He/She ....
3 If you want to use someone's camera for two hours, what do you say? Can I ....
....
4 What do you say to someone at 3 p.m.? Good ....
5 What do people do at a bus stop? They ....
6 What do you say to a friend if you need £1 for the phone? Can you ....
....
7 What do you say if someone makes too much noise? Please be ....

27.4 Answer these questions for *yourself*.

1 Are you expecting any visitors today?
2 What do you hope to do with this book?
3 Do you borrow things from your friends? What things?
4 Would you lend your best friend £200?

You can find other words that are often confused in these units in this book:
Do and **make**   Units 5 and 6
Take and **bring**   Units 8 and 9
Say and **tell**   Unit 13
Speak and **talk**   Unit 13
Rob and **steal**   Unit 57

28 Birth, marriage and death

A Birth

Diana **had a baby** yesterday.
It **was born** at 1.15 yesterday morning.
It **weighed** 3 kilograms.

They are going to **call** him John – after John, his grandfather.
Grandfather John's **birthday** is June 16th too – but he **was born** in 1945!
The baby's parents **were born** in 1974.

B Marriage

If you do not have a partner, you are **single**.
If you have a husband or wife, you are **married**.
If your husband or wife dies, you are **widowed**.
If your marriage breaks up, you are **separated/divorced** (the marriage has legally ended).

The wedding

bride   (bride)groom

Bill and Sarah **got married**.
Sarah **got married** to Bill. [NOT ~~with~~ Bill]
They (got) married in church.
They went on **honeymoon** to Italy.
They **were married** for twenty years.

C Death

Then Bill **became ill**.
He **died** last year.
He **died** of a heart attack.
Bill is **dead**.

The funeral

Exercises

28.1 When and where were you and your family and friends born? Write sentences about five people. *My mother was born in Scotland on July 4th 1947.*

28.2 When were these people born and when did they die? Write sentences.
1 Christopher Columbus (1451–1506) *Christopher Columbus was born in 1451 and died in 1506.*
2 Elvis Presley (1935–1977)
3 Genghis Khan (1162–1227)
4 Leonardo da Vinci (1452–1519)
5 George Washington (1732–1799)

28.3 Fill in the blanks with *died, dead* or *death*.
1 Jill's grandfather .... last year.
2 His .... was a great shock to her.
3 Her grandmother has been .... for five years now.
4 She .... of a heart attack.
5 Now all Jill's grandparents are ....

28.4 Find a word or phrase opposite which means.
1 the name for a woman on her wedding day. *bride*
2 the name for a man on his wedding day.
3 what you are if you haven't got a partner.
4 to be X kilograms.
5 what you are if your marriage has legally ended.
6 a religious service for a dead person.
7 a holiday after a wedding.
8 what you are if your husband or wife dies.

28.5 Fill the gaps with words from the box.

in	after	of	to	born	on

(1)............. 1993 Anne got married (2)............. Robert Smith. Unfortunately, Robert's grandmother, Rosemary Smith, died (3)............. old age soon after their wedding. Robert and Anne were (4)............. their honeymoon when she died. Anne's baby daughter was (5)............. two years later. They called the baby, Rosemary, (6)............. Robert's grandmother.

28.6 Write about your family. Use words and expressions from the opposite page.

29 The family

A family tree for some of Anne and Paul Mason's **relatives** or **relations**.

William + Mary Mason

Henry + Diana

Amelia   Anne + Paul   John   George + Sandra

Sarah   Jack   Emily   Peter

Paul is Anne's **husband** and Sarah and Jack's **father**.
Anne is Paul's **wife** and Sarah and Jack's **mother**.
Anne and Paul are Sarah and Jack's **parents**.
Sarah is Anne and Paul's **daughter**. Jack is their **son**.
Sarah is Jack's **sister**. Jack is Sarah's **brother**.
Henry is Sarah and Jack's **grandfather**. Diana is their **grandmother**.
Henry and Diana are Sarah and Jack's **grandparents**.
Sarah is Henry and Diana's **granddaughter**. Jack is their **grandson**.
John and George are Sarah and Jack's **uncles**.
Amelia and Sandra are Sarah and Jack's **aunts**.
Sarah is Amelia, John, George and Sandra's **niece**. Jack is their **nephew**.
Emily and Peter are Sarah and Jack's **cousins**.

Exercises

29.1 Look at the family tree on the opposite page. Finish the sentences.

1 Emily is Peter's ....*sister*...
2 Peter is Emily's ....
3 Anne is Emily's ....
4 Paul is Peter's ....
5 Diana is Peter's ....
6 Henry is Emily's ....
7 Peter is Paul's ....
8 Emily is Paul's ....
9 Sandra is Emily's ....
10 Sandra is George's ....
11 Sarah is Peter's ....

29.2 Draw your family tree. Then write sentences. Write about your relations. Anne is my mother.

29.3 The Masons have some other relatives. Finish the paragraph about them.

Fiona   Howard

Sandra has a brother, Howard. Howard is Peter's [1]................. Howard's wife is Emily's
[2].................... They are all very good friends. But Henry has a sister, Fiona. Henry is Fiona's
[3].................... Fiona does not get on well with William, her [4]................. but William loves
Fiona's three sons who are his [5].................... Fiona's boys are Paul's [6]................. but they
do not see each other very often. Then there is Anne's mother, Mrs Scott. She is Sarah and
Jack's [7].................... She and Anne, her [8]................., like to play golf together.

29.4 Ask a friend. Then write sentences about your friend and his or her family. Chen has one
brother and no sisters.

1 Have you got any brothers and sisters?
2 Have you got any cousins?
3 Have you got any nieces or nephews?
4 Have you got any grandparents?

29.5 Cover the page opposite. How many family words can you write down in two minutes?
Check what you wrote carefully with the book. Did you spell everything correctly? Which
words did you forget?

29.6 Write down the names of some people in your family. Then write down their relationship in
English to you. Use a dictionary if necessary.

30 Parts of the body

A Head and face

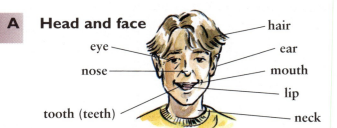

hair
eye
ear
nose
mouth
lip
tooth (teeth)
neck

B Arm and leg

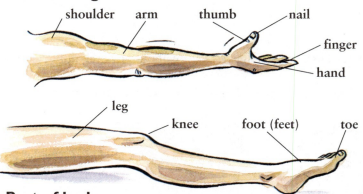

shoulder   arm   thumb   nail
finger
hand

leg   knee   foot (feet)   toe

C Rest of body

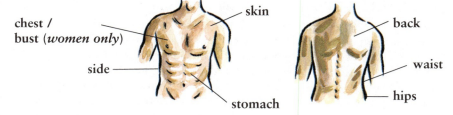

skin
chest /
bust (*women only*)
back
side
waist
stomach
hips

D Inside the body

 heart

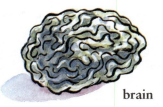 brain

 blood

E Pronunciation problems

eye /aɪ/   knee /niː/   stomach /ˈstʌmək/   heart /hɑːt/
blood /blʌd/   foot /fʊt/   tooth /tuːθ/

F Grammar

Usually we use my, your, his, her, etc. with parts of the body.
Jane is washing **her** hair. I have a pain in **my** leg.
[NOT Jane is washing ~~the~~ hair. NOT I have a pain in ~~the~~ leg.]

Exercises

30.1 **What are these parts of the body?**

1 eken *knee*   3 rathe   5 olderush   7 hotot
2 osen   4 hamcost   6 are

30.2 **Complete these sentences with words from the opposite page.**

1 A hand has five ....*fingers*......   5 The .... is a symbol of love.
2 A foot has five ....   6 You hear with your ....
3 An adult has 32 ....   7 The child sat on her dad's ....
4 You smell with your ....   8 Your .... type can be A, B, AB or O.

30.3 **Parts of the body words are used in different contexts too.**

1 A chair has arms, legs and a back. What do you think they are?
2 This is a needle. Where is its eye?
3 This is a clock. Where is its face? Where are its hands?
4 This is a bottle. Where is its neck?
5 This is a mountain. Where is its foot?

30.4 **Parts of the body are often used in compound nouns too. Complete these nouns with a word from the opposite page.**

1 ....*arm*.chair   3 ....stick   5 ....scarf

2 ....ball   4 ....brush   6 ....bag

30.5 Write down six of the words from the opposite page together with the same words in your own language. Then write down six different words with a picture of what the word means. Next week, test yourself. Which group of words do you remember best – those which you learnt with a translation or those which you learnt with a picture?

31 Clothes

A Clothes

hat coat jacket scarf gloves shoes trainers boots suit

socks skirt tie

T-shirt watch shirt dress ring belt sweater/ jumper

B Plural words

These words are always plural in English. They need a plural verb.

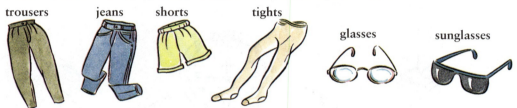

trousers jeans shorts tights glasses sunglasses

My suit is new but these trousers are old. Her shorts/jeans/tights are blue.
Note: You say: a pair of shorts/glasses/trousers, etc.

C Verbs

You **wear** clothes but you **carry** things. [NOT you ~~use~~ clothes]

Naomi **is wearing** a long red coat. She's **carrying** a suitcase
and a small handbag.
You can also say: Naomi **has** (**got**) a red coat **on**.
You **carry** a briefcase and an umbrella.

In the morning you **get dressed** or **put** your
clothes **on**. At night you **get undressed**
or **take your clothes off**.

Tip: Can you name all the clothes you usually wear? If not, use a dictionary to help
you find the words you need.

Exercises

31.1   Put these words into one or both columns.

	men	*women*
coat jacket dress tie belt shoes watch suit skirt shirt ring trousers sweater T-shirt handbag briefcase	*coat*	*coat*

31.2   Match the part of the body with the item of clothing.

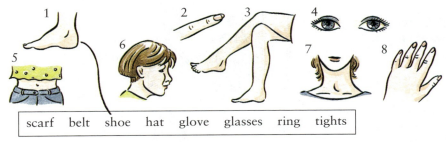

| scarf   belt   shoe   hat   glove   glasses   ring   tights |

31.3   Choose one of the verbs in the box and put it in the right form.

| be   wear   carry   have |

1   John's jeans ....*are*........ blue and his T-shirt .... red.
2   Julia .... jeans and a T-shirt today.
3   Meena .... got a red coat on and she .... some flowers. Where is she
    going?
4   Sarah's dress .... old but her shoes .... new.
5   Last year John's trousers .... white. Now they .... grey.
6   .... this a new pair of jeans?

31.4   Look at the picture and write
the names next to the numbers.

31.5   Write a paragraph about what you are wearing today.

*I'm wearing a white T-shirt and a blue jumper. I've got a pair of black trousers on. I'm
wearing blue socks and white trainers. I've also got a watch and a pair of glasses on.*

32 Describing people

Describing people

A Height /haɪt/ (= how many metres?)

Mary Pimm is a very **tall** woman.
[NOT Mary Pimm is a very ~~high~~ woman.]

Tom Jakes is quite **short**.
[NOT Tom Jakes is quite ~~low~~.]

Mary Pimm   Tom Jakes

If you aren't tall or short, you are **medium height**.
To ask if someone is tall or short, we say:
How tall is Mary/Tom? She's 1.60 metres tall. / He's 1.48 metres tall.

B Weight /weɪt/
(= how many kilos?)

Dolly Ryan

Dolly Ryan is really **slim**.
I was very **thin** when I was in hospital.
  (**thin** is a more negative word)

A rather **fat** man opened the door. (**fat** is quite negative)
The doctor said I am **overweight**. (= more kilos than is good for me)
How much do you weigh? I weigh 62 kilos / 74 kilos, etc.

C Face and head

Sally has **dark** hair and **dark skin**.
  She has **brown** eyes.
Polly has **blonde** (or **fair**) hair and **fair skin**.
  She has **blue** eyes.
Billy has **a beard** and **long** hair.
  He has **green** eyes.
Harry has **a moustache** and **short** hair. /məˈstæʃ/

You can also use **has got**, for example, Sally **has got** dark hair and dark skin.

D Age

My grandmother is 97. She's very **old**. My sister is 14. She's **young**, but would like to be **older**. My father is 56. He's **middle-aged**, but would like to be **younger**!

This hospital is for **elderly** people. (more polite than **old**)

E Looks: positive (+) and negative (-)

My sister is quite **pretty**. (+++) (usually girls/women only). She's a very **beautiful** girl.
  (++++) Jim's a very **handsome** man. (++++) (usually for men only) Bob's a rather **ugly**
  man. (---)
I'm not ugly or beautiful, I'm just **ordinary-looking**! (+/-)

Exercises

32.1 Fill the gaps in the sentences.

1 He's only one metre 52. He's quite ...*short*.....
2 Very .... people are often good at basketball.
3 Models are usually ....
4 Is her skin dark? No it's ....
5 She's only 12. She's very ....
6 If I eat too much I'll be ....
7 My grandmother is in this hospital. It's a hospital for .... people. (don't use 'old')

32.2 Ask questions for these answers. Use the words in brackets.

1 ....*How tall is your brother?*............ (your brother)
  He's about one metre 75.
2 Is ....? (Elena's hair)
  No, her hair's dark.
3 Is ....? (Mike's hair)
  Yes, it is quite long.
4 Are ....? (your parents)
  Not really, they're middle-aged.
5 Is .... ? (his sister)
  Yes, all the boys want to go out with her.
6 Why ....? (Sara – thin)
  She has been very ill.

32.3 Write sentences describing the people in these pictures.

Suzanna

Jeff

Caroline

Dick

1 Suzanna's got ....
2 Jeff has ....
3 Caroline's got ....
4 Dick's hair is .... and he ....

32.4 Write down the names of three people you know. Then write about:

– their height (tall, short, medium height)
– their hair (colour, long, short, beard)
– their eyes (colour)
– their looks (ordinary, handsome, etc.)

33 Health and illness

A How are you today?

I am **very well**, thanks. I'm **fine**, thanks.
I **don't feel very well**. I must go home and rest. (I'll probably be OK tomorrow.)
I **feel ill**. Can you get **a doctor** please. (Perhaps a serious problem.)
That fish was bad. I think I'm going to be **sick!** (I want to vomit.)

B Everyday problems

Have you got **an aspirin**? I've **got a headache**. /ˈhedeɪk/

I've got **toothache**. I need to go to the dentist. /ˈtuːθeɪk/

I'm going to bed with a hot drink. I've **got a cold**.

C Problems people have for many years / all their lives

I get **hay-fever** every summer, from flowers and grass. I **sneeze** all day. /ˈheɪfiːvə/

My little brother has **asthma**;
    sometimes he can't breathe. /ˈæsmə/

sneeze

D Illnesses in hot/tropical countries

mosquito

In some countries, mosquitoes can give people **malaria**. /məˈleɜrɪə/
The drinking water was bad, and many children had **cholera**. /ˈkɒlɜrə/

E Serious illnesses

My father **had a heart attack**.
    He is **in hospital**.
Cancer kills many people who
    smoke ever year. /ˈkænsə/

F How to keep fit and well

Have a good **diet**: eat lots of fruit and vegetables.
Get some exercise: swimming, jogging, cycling are good for you.
Don't have too much **stress**: relax after work, and don't panic about work!

Exercises

33.1 Put these health problems in the three columns. Do you think they are *not serious*, *more serious* or *very serious*?

cancer   toothache   cholera   hay-fever   a headache
a heart attack   a cold   asthma

not serious	more serious	very serious
a headache		

33.2 Complete the dialogues.

1 A: How are you today?
B: ....
A: Good!

2 A: Are you OK?
B: No, ...
A: Would you like to use the bathroom?
B: Yes, thank you.

3 A: I ....
B: Shall I call a doctor?
A: Yes, I think you should.

4 A: ....
B: Here's the phone number of the school's dentist.
A: Thanks.

5 A: Your nose is red. Have you got ....?
B: Yes.
A: Have a hot drink and go to bed early.

33.3 Answer these questions for yourself. Use a dictionary if you have to.

1 What do you think is a good diet?
2 What sort of exercise do you like?
3 Do you have a lot of stress in your life?
4 Have you ever been in hospital?

33.4 What illnesses are connected with ...

1 a mosquito bite? malaria
2 bad drinking water?
3 pollution, traffic fumes?
4 grass, flowers, etc.?
5 smoking?

34 Feelings

Love / like / hate

love   like   don't like   hate
(dislike)

I **love** my family and my best friend.
I **like** my job.
I **don't like** horror films. (I **dislike** (horror films) is less common.)
I **hate** my boss.

I **prefer** coffee **to** tea. (= I like coffee more than I like tea.)

I **want** (= I would like) **a new car**. (want + noun)
I **want to buy** a new car. (want + infinitive)
Note: I **want my father to buy** a new car. (verb + object + infinitive) [NOT ~~I want that~~ …]

I **hope to do** well in my exam. (hope + infinitive)
I **hope** (**that**) my friend does well in his exam. (hope + that clause)

B **Happy / sad / tired**

happy   angry   sad   surprised

hungry   thirsty   upset   tired

ill   well

cold   warm   hot

Exercises

34.1 Do you love, like, not like or hate these things? Write sentences.

1 chocolate   5 football
2 cowboy films   6 cats
3 aeroplanes   7 cars
4 tea   8 jazz music

34.2 Which do you prefer – tea or coffee? Write answers as in the example.

1 tea or coffee? *I prefer coffee to tea.*   4 BMWs or Rolls Royces?
2 dogs or cats?   5 strawberry or chocolate ice-cream?
3 sunbathing or sightseeing?   6 watching sport or doing sport?

34.3 Answer these questions using *want* or *hope*.

1 You're thirsty. What do you want? *I want a cup of tea.*
2 The lesson feels very long. What do you hope?
3 You're hungry. What do you want?
4 Your friend feels ill. What do you hope?
5 You're tired. What do you want?
6 You're upset. What do you want?
7 It is very cold weather. What do you hope?

34.4 Look at the pictures. How do they feel? Use one of the words from B opposite.

1 Diana .... *is hungry.* ....

2 Fred ....

3 The children ....

4 William ....

5 Mrs Jones ....

6 Mr Jones ....

7 Fiona ....

34.5 When did you last feel ...

1 angry? 2 surprised? 3 upset?
I felt angry this morning when I read the newspaper.

35 Greetings and other useful phrases

A **Every day**   good morning   good afternoon   good evening

When we leave someone we usually both say **Goodbye** and perhaps, **See you soon! See you soon** is quite informal.

When someone goes to bed, we usually say **Goodnight**. We sometimes also say **Sleep well**. Don't say **Goodnight** when you arrive somewhere, only when you leave.

If you ask for something you usually say **Please**.

If someone does something nice for you, you say **Thank you**.

B **Special days**

When it is someone's birthday we say **Happy Birthday** [NOT ~~Congratulations~~].

On (or near to) the 25th December (Christmas Day) we say **Happy** or **Merry Christmas**. /ˈkrɪsməs/

On (or near to) the 1st January (New Year's Day) we say **Happy New Year**.

If someone is going to do something difficult (for example, take an exam or have an interview for a job) we say **Good luck!**

If someone has done something special (for example, done well in an exam, got a new job, had a baby) we say **Congratulations!** or **Well done!**

Exercises

35.1 **Choose one of the phrases from the opposite page to fit the dialogues.**

1 A: *(sneezes)* Atchoo!
   B: ....

2 A: I'm taking my driving test today.
   B: ....

3 A: I passed my driving test!
   B: ....

4 A: Goodbye.
   B: ....

5 A: It's my birthday today.
   B: ....

6 A: How are you?
   B: ....

7 A: Hello!
   B: ....

8 A: Here's your tea.
   B: ....

35.2 **What is the person saying in the pictures?**

35.3 **What do you say? Choose a phrase opposite.**

1 You want to order a coffee. The waiter is reading the newspaper.
2 A friend buys you a drink.
3 A child says 'Goodnight' to you.
4 You answer the phone at work. It is 10.30 a.m.
5 You answer the phone at work. It is 3 p.m.
6 It is 2 a.m. on January 1st. You meet a friend on the street.
7 A friend spoke too quickly. You don't understand.
8 It is 24th December. You meet a friend on the bus.

35.4 **Ann and Bill meet in a bar. Bill usually says the wrong thing. Correct his mistakes.**

ANN: Good evening.
BILL: Good day.
ANN: How are you?
BILL: Terrible. I've got a bad cold and …
ANN: It's my birthday today.
BILL: Congratulations.

ANN: Would you like a drink?
BILL: No, thank you. A coke.
ANN: With ice?
BILL: No, please.
ANN: Here you are. Cheers.
BILL: Bless you!

35.5 **Write a conversation using as many as possible of the phrases from the opposite page.**

36 Countries, languages and people

All the nouns and adjectives in this unit always begin with a capital letter, for example Africa [NOT africa].

A The Continents

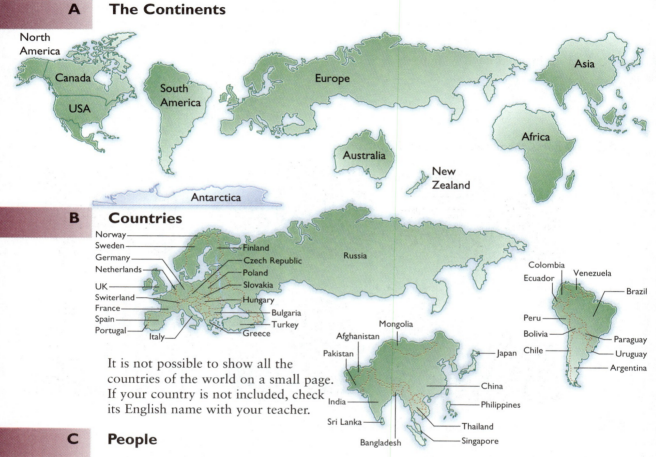

B Countries

It is not possible to show all the countries of the world on a small page. If your country is not included, check its English name with your teacher.

C People

notes	adjective
Most country adjectives end in *(i)an*.	German, Mexican, Jamaican, Russian, Canadian, Australian, Brazilian, Egyptian, Peruvian, Korean, Argentinian
Many country adjectives end in *ish*.	British, English, Irish, Scottish, Polish, Swedish, Finnish, Spanish, Turkish
A few country adjectives end in *ese*.	Chinese, Portuguese, Japanese, Vietnamese, Nepalese

Exceptions: French (from France), Dutch (from Holland), Swiss (from Switzerland), Greek, Iraqi, Thai, Icelandic, Arab, Israeli

D Languages and people

Words for languages are usually the same as the 'people' adjective: **English, French, Japanese, Thai, Spanish, Chinese, Norwegian** (from **Norway**), etc. There is one exception: **Arabic**.

Exercises

You may need to ask a teacher or to use a dictionary to help you with some of these exercises – it is not possible to include every country and nationality on the left-hand page.

36.1 In which continents are these places?

1 Mount Everest Asia
2 The Sahara
3 The Amazon
4 Wogga Wogga
5 The Volga
6 Mount Kilimanjaro
7 The Mississippi
8 Mount Fuji
9 Lake Titicaca

36.2 Which countries are these ? Write their names on them.

Brazil   Spain   Russia   China   Sweden   Thailand

36.3 Where are these capital cities? Write sentences.

1 Tokyo Tokyo is the capital of Japan.
2 Rome
3 Canberra
4 Bogota
5 Cairo
6 Vienna
7 Edinburgh
8 Ankara
9 Buenos Aires
10 Madrid

36.4 Write down in English:

1 the name of your country.
2 the names of the countries next to your country.
3 the names of any other countries which are important for your country in some way.
4 the word for your language.
5 the name for people from your country.

36.5 Which country is different? (Think of the languages they speak there.) Write sentences.

1 England, Canada, Iceland, Australia In England, Canada and Australia they speak English but in Iceland they speak Icelandic.
2 Mexico, Brazil, Spain, Chile
3 Italy, Austria, Germany, Switzerland
4 Morocco, Egypt, China, Saudi Arabia
5 Switzerland, Canada, Scotland, France

36.6 What is the adjective for these countries?

1 Cuba Cuban
2 Vietnam
3 Korea
4 Thailand
5 Iraq
6 Germany
7 Egypt
8 Argentina
9 Holland
10 Spain
11 Peru
12 China
13 Britain
14 Greece
15 Australia
16 Poland
17 India

37 Weather

A **Types of weather**

sun   rain   cloud   snow

fog   wind   thunder   lightning

B **Adjectives and verbs**

noun	adjective
sun	sunny
rain	rainy
wind	windy
cloud	cloudy
snow	snowy
fog	foggy
thunder	thundery
lightning	–

It's a sunny day in Tokyo today, but it's cloudy in Hong Kong.
It's foggy in Sydney and it's snowing / snowy in Moscow.
It's raining in Barcelona but the sun is shining in Granada.

It's lovely weather today, isn't it! [NOT It's ~~a~~ lovely weather.]
It's a horrible day, isn't it!

You cannot say It's ~~winding~~ / ~~clouding~~ / ~~fogging~~ / ~~sunning~~.

C **Other useful weather words**

It is very **hot** in Mexico – it is often **45 degrees** there in summer.
It is very **cold** in the Arctic – it is often **minus 50 degrees** there.
It is very **wet** in London – carry an umbrella when you go sightseeing there.
It is very **dry** in the Sahara – it doesn't often rain there.
A **hurricane** is a very strong wind.
A **storm** is when there is a strong wind and rain together.
A **thunderstorm** is when there is thunder, lightning, rain and sometimes wind together.

> **Tip:** If you are able to see the weather forecast in English on television, watch it as often as you can.

Exercises

37.1 Match the words and the symbols.

1 snow   2 sun   3 rain   4 fog   5 lightning   6 wind   7 cloud

a   b   d   g

f   c   e

37.2 Look at the types of weather in A. Write them down in order from your most favourite to your least favourite.

37.3 Look at the chart. Write sentences about the towns in the chart.

Hanoi   1 It is sunny in Hanoi. ....

Hong Kong   2 It is raining in Hong Kong. ....

La Paz   3 It is ....

Paris   4 It ....

Tashkent   5 ....

Seoul   6 ....

Warsaw   7 ....

Washington   8 ....

37.4 Complete these sentences with a word from the opposite page.

1 The sun .... every day last month.
2 When it ...., I take my umbrella.
3 It is lovely .... today, isn't it.
4 When it ...., we can go skiing.
5 You see .... before you hear thunder.
6 It is 24 .... here today.
7 It is dangerous to be in a small boat at sea in a ....
8 It is very .... in Siberia in winter.

37.5 Are these sentences true about the weather in your country? If not, correct them.

1 It often snows in December.
2 It is usually 40 degrees in summer and minus 20 degrees in winter.
3 There are thunderstorms every day in August.
4 It is very wet in spring.
5 We never have hurricanes.
6 Summer is my favourite season because it is usually hot and dry.

37.6 Write about the weather where you are today. Use as many words as possible from the opposite page.

38 In the town

A The town centre

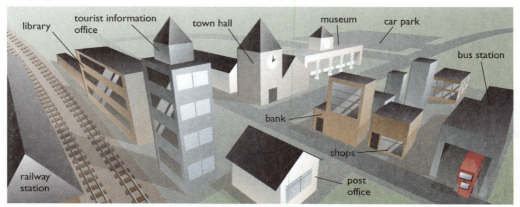

You can **get a train** at the **railway station**.
You can **change money** at the **bank**.
You can **read books** and **newspapers** at the **library**. /ˈlaɪbrərɪ/ *or* /ˈlaɪbrɪ/
You can **park your car** in/at the **car park**.

B Streets and roads

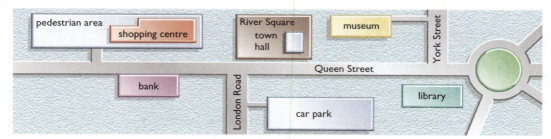

Asking for help

Where is the main square? /skweə/ **How do I get to** X street? **Is there** a pedestrian area here? /pəˈdestrɪən/ **Can I park here? Excuse me, I'm looking for** the museum.

C People in the town

police officer   traffic warden /ˈwɔːdən/   shop assistant   librarian   bank clerk

D Signs

no parking   no entry   bus stop   crossroads   traffic lights

Exercises

38.1 Answer the questions.

1 Where can I get a bus to London? *At the bus station.*
2 Where can I get information about hotels?
3 Where can I change money?
4 Where can I park?
5 Where can I see very old things?
6 Where can I post a letter?

38.2 Look at the map on the opposite page. Ask questions.

1 *Where's the library?* .... Near the roundabout.
2 .... In the square.
3 .... Go left at York Street.
4 .... Yes , in the pedestrian area.
5 .... London Road car park is best.
6 .... There's a bank in Queen Street.

38.3 What words are these?

1 sumuem *museum*
2 nowt hlal   5 ywrlaai nttoisa
3 brilyra   6 dtaeepsrin raae
4 rac prak   7 frtafci dnearw

38.4 What are these signs?

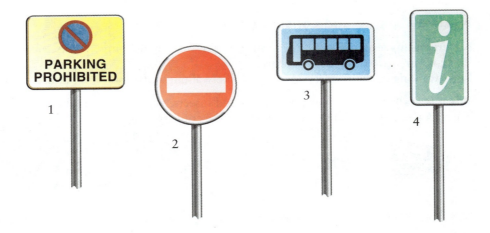

38.5 Write a paragraph about your town. Use the words opposite.

39 In the countryside

The **countryside** and the **country** both mean 'not the city'. **Country** can also mean a nation (e.g. France, China).

A Things we can see in the countryside

B Living and working in the countryside

In the countryside, people usually live in a **small town** (e.g. 6,000 people) or **village** /ˈvɪlɪdʒ/ (e.g. 700 people).
A **farmer** lives **on a farm** and works in the fields.
My friend lives in a **cottage** /ˈkɒtɪdʒ/ (small house in a village or out in the countryside).

C Nature /ˈneɪtʃə/ and conservation /ˌkɒnsəˈveɪʃn/

Nature means 'everything in the natural world' (= animals, birds, plants, etc.).
I love **nature**. [NOT I love ~~the~~ nature.]
I like walking **in the countryside**. [NOT I like walking in the ~~nature~~. 'Nature' is not a place.]

When we talk about animals, birds, fish and insects, we can say **wildlife**.
There is wonderful **wildlife** in the north of the country.

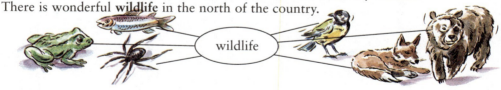

Near the village there is **a conservation area** (= place where wildlife and nature are protected).
In the south of the country, there is a **national park** (= very big national conservation area).

D Things to do in the countryside

You can take food and drink and have **a picnic**.
You can **go walking/skiing** in the mountains.

Exercises

39.1 Cover the left-hand page. How many names of things in the countryside can you remember?

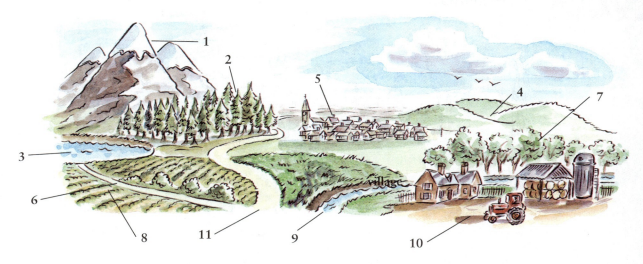

39.2 Fill the gaps in thse sentences.

1 My brother is a ...farmer......... He lives .... a farm.
2 It's not a big house; it's just a ....
3 The farm is near a ....; it has 800 people.
4 20 kilometres from the village there is a small .... It has 9,000 people.

39.3 Match the beginning of the sentences on the left with the ends of the sentences on the right. Draw lines.

1 We went swimming	sitting by the river.
2 We went walking	in the national park.
3 We went skiing	in the lake. The water was warm.
4 We saw some wonderful wildlife	along a 5-kilometre path.
5 We had a picnic	down the mountain.

39.4 Describe the typical countryside where you come from. Write four sentences about it. Use these questions to help you.

1 Are there any woods or forests?
2 Are there any hills or mountains?
3 Are there any lakes or rivers?
4 Are there many villages or small towns?
5 Are there farms?
6 Are there paths where you can walk?
7 Can you go skiing?
8 Can you see wildlife?

39.5 Put *the* in the sentence if necessary.

1 He loves .... nature.
2 She wants to live in .... country.
3 They are interested in .... wildlife.

40 Animals and pets

Farm animals

animal	produce	baby
horse		foal
cow	milk, leather, meat (beef)	calf
sheep	wool, meat (lamb)	lamb
pig	meat (pork, bacon, ham)	piglet
hen	eggs, meat (chicken)	chick

B **Wild or zoo animals**

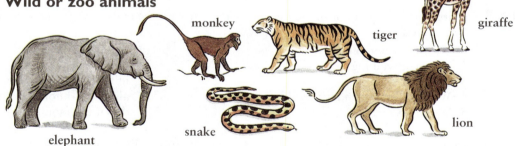

C **Pets**

These animals are often **pets**.

Parrots and budgies are **birds**.
You **take** your dog **for a walk** but you don't usually take your cat for a walk.

Exercises

40.1 Complete these sentences.

1 A .....*tortoise*..... goes to sleep in winter.
2 A .... has a very long neck.
3 ...., ... and .... are birds.
4 .... and .... are large cats.
5 You can ride a .... and an ....
6 .... swim and .... fly.
7 You can buy .... at a butcher's.
8 .... and .... give us things for breakfast.

40.2 Match the animal with its meat and with its young animal. Draw lines.

animal	meat	young
sheep	chicken	piglet
cow	pork	lamb
hen	beef	calf
pig	lamb	chick

40.3 Look at the animals opposite. Which of them …

1 eat meat?
2 give us things that we wear?
3 produce their babies in eggs?

40.4 Look at the pictures and complete the crossword.

Across
3
6
7
8

Down
1
2
4
5
9

40.5 There are 17 different animals in the pictures on the opposite page. Cover the page. How many of these animals can you remember?

41 Travelling

A Types of transport

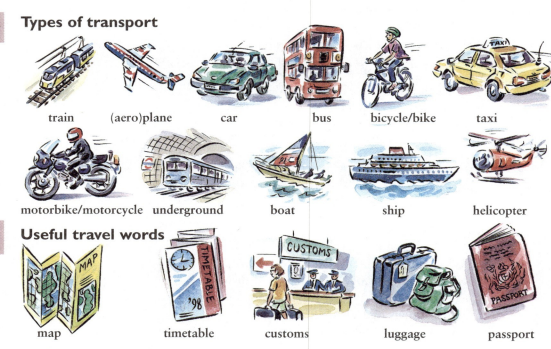

train   (aero)plane   car   bus   bicycle/bike   taxi

motorbike/motorcycle   underground   boat   ship   helicopter

B Useful travel words

map   timetable   customs   luggage   passport

Can I have a **single/return** (ticket) to Barcelona please? (single = Madrid → Barcelona; return = Madrid ⇄ Barcelona)

I'd like to **book/reserve a seat in advance.** (to make sure you have a seat)

How much is the (train / bus / taxi / air) **fare**?

Was the **journey** long? [NOT Was the ~~travel~~ long?]

C By train

The train **arriving at** platform 3 is the 16:50 train to Paris.

The Edinburgh train **departs/leaves from** platform 6.

Is there a **buffet/restaurant car** on this train?

Do I have to **change trains** for Toulouse? (= get off one train and go onto another)

D By plane

You have to **check in** an hour before the plane **takes off** (= leaves the ground).

I **went through customs** but nobody **checked** my passport. [NOT ~~controlled~~ my passport]
(See Unit 27.)

Give your **boarding card** to the **flight stewards** when you get on the plane.

Have a good **flight**.

The plane **landed** in New York at 5.30.

E By car

We **hired a car** for a week. We had to **fill** it **up with petrol**.

Can I **give** you **a lift**? I'm going into town.

Unit 14 (Moving) has some more useful words about travelling.

Exercises

41.1 Match the words on the left with their definitions on the right. Draw lines.

1	land	a a place to eat on a train
2	fare	b bags and suitcases
3	buffet car	c it says when trains depart and arrive
4	ship	d what you must pay when you travel
5	timetable	e planes do this at airports
6	platform	f it travels on water. e.g. the *Titanic*
7	luggage	g where you stand when you are waiting for a train

41.2 Can you answer these questions about the vocabulary of travel?

1 What is the difference between a single ticket and a return ticket?
2 What does a customs officer do?
3 Does a plane take off at the end of a journey?
4 What do you do with a boarding card?
5 What is the difference between hiring a car and buying a car?
6 If you ask someone for a lift, do you want to go to the top floor?

41.3 Here are instructions to get to John's house from the airport.

When you arrive at the airport, take a number 10 bus to the railway station. Then take a train to Bigtown. The journey takes half an hour and you get off the train at the second stop. Take a taxi from the station to John's house.

Now write instructions for someone to get to your house from the airport.

41.4 Make cards to test yourself. Write the word on one side of the card and a picture (or a definition or translation) on the other side. Look at the pictures (or definitions or translations). Can you remember the English words?

41.5 Complete the crossword.

Across

3
6
7
8

Down

1
2
3
4
5

42 Notices

No smoking here.

You go out here.

You go in here.

There are lots of different signs for public toilets.

Men   Women

Toilets   WC

Tip: Look for other signs in English. Write down any that you see.

Exercises

42.1 Choose the correct letter.

1 Your sister wants to go to the toilet.
2 You want to buy something.
3 Your father wants to go to the toilet.
4 You want to go out of the shop.

42.2 Look at each of the notices on the opposite page. Write down a place where you can see each of them. No smoking — in a restaurant.

42.3 Look at the pictures and answer the questions.

1 Can you go in now? No.

2 Can you use the telephone now?

3 Can you park your car here?

4 How do you open the door – a or b?

5 How do you open the door – a or b?

6 You haven't got much money. Is this a
   good time to go shopping?

42.4 Notices often give you information (for example, that a shop is closed) or give you instructions (for example, that smoking is forbidden). Put the notices on the opposite page into two columns – *Information* and *Instructions*.

42.5 Where can you find examples of signs in English in your country?

43 Food and drink

A Everyday food

Do you want some **bread**?
  [NOT Do you want ~~a~~ bread?]
In China, most people eat **rice**.
In Italy, **pasta** is very popular.
Many people eat **meat** or **fish** almost every day.

B Popular food / fast food

Most young people love **hot-dogs**,
hamburgers and **pizzas**.

Most British people like **fish and chips**.

C Fruit and vegetables /ˈvedʒtəbəlz/

Vegetables are good for you. **Fruit** is also good for you. (singular) [NOT fruit~~s~~]

Vegetables

carrots   beans   potatoes   tomatoes   peas   onions /ˈʌnjənz/   garlic   mushrooms

Fruit   apple

orange /ˈɒrɪndʒ/   banana   pear /peə/   grapes   strawberries /ˈstrɔːbrɪz/   pineapple /ˈpaɪnæpl/

D Drinks

tea   coffee   milk   fruit juice   beer   wine   mineral water

Tip: Go to a supermarket. How many drinks and foods have English names on them? Try to learn some of them.

Exercises

43.1 Complete the sentences. Use words from A and B opposite.

1 ....*Rice*........ is the most important food in Japan.
2 .... and .... are very popular in Britain.
3 Chips are made from ....
4 Most Italian people love ....
5 Hamburgers are made from ....
6 A .... is a sausage inside a piece of bread.

43.2 Put these words into two lists: fruit and vegetables, as in the example.

beans   pineapple   grapes   onions   apple   carrot   garlic   pear   mushrooms

fruit	*vegetables*
	beans

43.3 Write the names of these fruit and vegetables.

1 .... 3 .... 5 ....

2 .... 4 .... 6 ....

43.4 Here are the names of some drinks with the letters mixed up. What are they?

1 eta **tea**   4 fecofe
2 rebe   5 rituf eciju
3 klim   6 nilemar retaw

43.5 What are your four favourite foods? And your three favourite drinks? Are they good for you? Use a dictionary if the names are not in this unit.

44 In the kitchen

A **What's in the kitchen?**

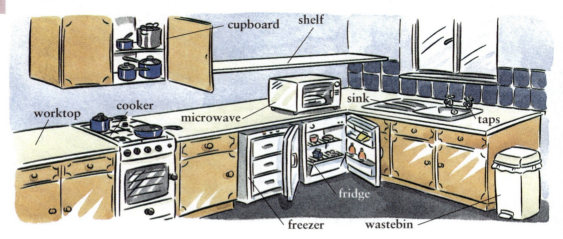

B **Things we use in the kitchen**

C **Things we use for eating and drinking**

D **Questions in the kitchen**

Where can I find a mug / cloth / some kitchen paper?
Can I help with the washing-up / the cooking?
Where does this cup / plate / frying pan **go**? (where do you keep it?)
Where shall I put this cup / the milk?

Exercises

44.1 Tick (✓) *yes* or *no*.

		yes	no
1	I use a frying pan to drink out of.		✓
2	Washing-up liquid makes the dishes clean.		
3	The fridge is cold inside.		
4	The freezer is not as cold as the fridge.		
5	I turn on the tap to get water.		
6	A tea towel is for making plates wet.		

44.2 Ask questions for these answers. Use words from the left-hand page.

1 .... It's in the cupboard.
2 .... It's on the cooker.
3 .... Please put it in the sink.
4 .... Thanks. You can wash those plates, and I'll
dry them.

44.3 What do you need?

1 To make coffee I need ... *coffee, water, milk, a coffee maker, a cup, a spoon.* ....
2 To make tea I need ....
3 To fry an egg I need ....
4 To eat my food I need ....
5 To drink some water I need ....
6 To make my dinner in just two minutes I need ....

44.4 Look at the pictures. Answer the questions.

1 What's near the cooker?
2 What's on the cooker?
3 What's on the shelf?
4 What's in the cupboard?

45 In the bedroom and bathroom

A Bedroom

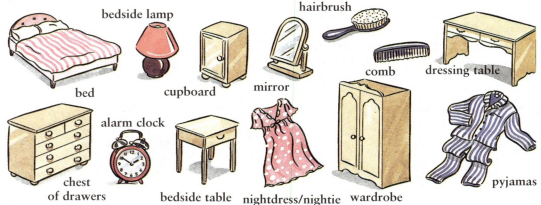

bedside lamp

hairbrush

bed

cupboard

mirror

comb

dressing table

chest of drawers

alarm clock

bedside table

nightdress/nightie

wardrobe

pyjamas

B Bathroom

soap

toothpaste

shelf

toothbrush

shower

bath

basin

towel

shampoo

toilet

C Joel's routine

Joel goes to bed at 11 o'clock. He goes upstairs to his bedroom.
He gets undressed and goes to bed.
He reads for a bit. He turns off the light and falls asleep.
He wakes up when his alarm clock rings.
He gets up. He has a shower, cleans his teeth and gets dressed.
He goes downstairs to the kitchen for breakfast.
(See Unit 12.)

Exercises

45.1 Look at the picture and write the words next to the numbers.

45.2 Write down five more things that you need to take with you if you go to stay with a friend for one night.

.... toothbrush ....

....

45.3 Look at the pictures. Describe what the people are doing.

1 Anne ...is cleaning her teeth............ 4 Mr Park ....

2 Selim and Umit .... 5 Jaime ....

3 Mrs Park .... 6 Lee ....

45.4 Write down the words for all the things you have in your bathroom. Use a dictionary to help you, if you need to.

45.5 Describe your bedroom. Write four or five sentences.

45.6 Write about your night-time routine. Use the verbs in C opposite. *I usually go to bed at ...*

46 In the living room

A Things in the living room

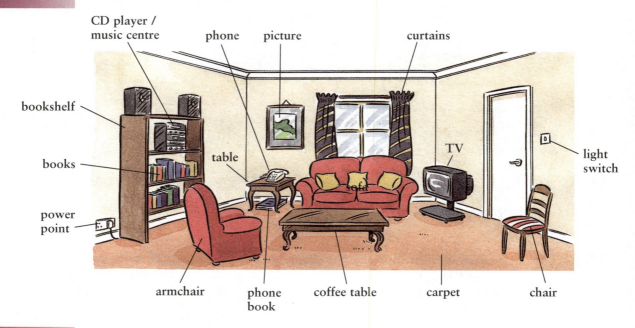

CD player /
music centre

phone

picture

curtains

bookshelf

books

table

TV

light
switch

power
point

armchair

phone
book

coffee table

carpet

chair

B Useful prepositions

The sofa is **near** the window.
Next to the sofa is a small table.
The TV is **in the corner**.

The coffee table is **in the middle** of the room.
The bookshelf is **against** the wall.
Where's the telephone book? **Under** the small table.

C Things we do in the living room

Every evening I **watch television**.
Sometimes I **listen to the radio** or **listen to music**.
Sometimes I **read**.
Sometimes I just **relax**. (= rest and do nothing)

D Things we use

Where is **the remote control** for the TV?
There's **a reading lamp** on the desk.
Close the curtains and **switch the light on**; it's getting dark.
Turn the radio off and **turn the TV on**, please. I want to watch the football.

Exercises

46.1 Write down the names of ...

1 Somewhere you can put books. **a bookshelf**
2 Somewhere two/three people can sit.
3 Somewhere you can put down your coffee-cup.
4 Something you can look at on the wall.
5 Something for switching the light on/off.
6 Something for listening to music.
7 Something under your feet.

46.2 Choose (a), (b) or (c).

1 If you want to relax, which is the best?
   (a) a chair   (b) an armchair   (c) a sofa
2 If it is dark and you want to read, do you ...?
   (a) close the curtains   (b) switch on the reading lamp   (c) switch off the light
3 If you want to watch a different TV station, do you ...?
   (a) use the remote control   (b) use the power point   (c) turn off the TV

46.3 Fill the gaps with the correct prepositions. Look at the picture opposite.

1 .... the floor there is a carpet.
2 There is a small table .... the corner. There is a TV .... the table.
3 The TV is .... the door.
4 The bookshelf is .... the wall.
5 The coffee table is .... front .... the sofa.

46.4 Write about your living room at home. Draw a plan of it first.

Describe your furniture (tables, chairs, sofa, etc.). Say where things are (e.g. next to ..., in the corner ..., near ..., etc.). What colour are the walls? Are there any pictures on them? What do you do when you are in your living room?

46.5 Word puzzle. How many names of things in the living room can you find?

t	e	n	b	w	o
a	c	h	a	i	r
b	a	x	b	n	r
l	r	c	o	d	a
e	p	v	o	o	d
m	e	s	k	w	i
h	t	v	s	u	o

47 Jobs

A What's his/her job?

doctor

teacher

nurse

mechanic

secretary

shop assistant

hairdresser

engineer

farmer

B Job (noun) and work (verb) /wɜːk/

What's your **job**? *or* What do you **do**?
I'm a waiter.

Where do you **work**? I work in a restaurant.
Is it an interesting **job**? Yes, I like it.

C Workplaces

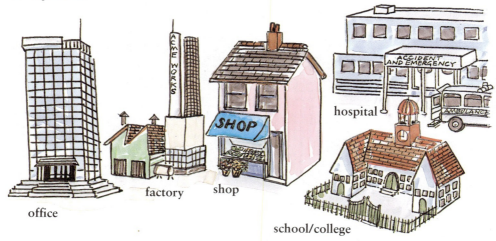

office

factory

shop

hospital

school/college

I work **in** a factory / an office etc. I work **at/from** home.

Exercises

47.1 **Where do they work?**

1 A teacher _....works in a school/college/university.._
2 A doctor _..._
3 A waiter _..._
4 A secretary _.._
5 A shop assistant _..._
6 A hairdresser _..._

47.2 **Match the pictures with the jobs in the box.**

| farmer   engineer   taxi-driver   mechanic   nurse   secretary |

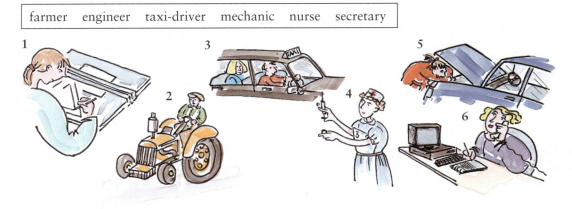

47.3 **Answer the questions for *yourself*.**

1 What do you do?
2 Where do you work?
3 Is it an interesting job?

47.4 **Word puzzle. Fill in the letters.**

Across
1 works on a bus
2 works in a school
3 writes books

Down
1 works in a hospital
2 works in a restaurant
3 works with the doctor

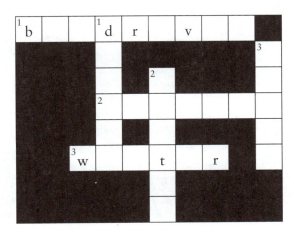

48 At school and university

A Subjects

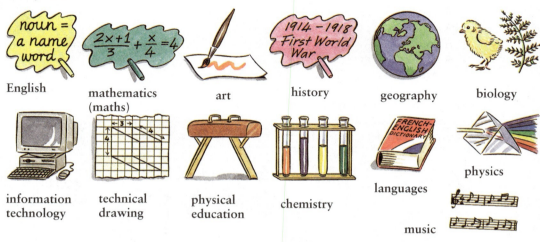

English

mathematics (maths)

art

history

geography

biology

information technology

technical drawing

physical education

chemistry

languages

physics

music

B Useful things

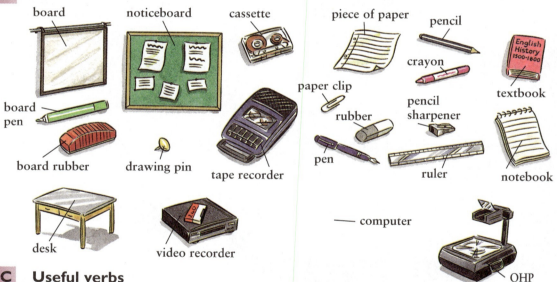

board

noticeboard

cassette

piece of paper

pencil

crayon

board pen

paper clip

rubber

pencil sharpener

textbook

board rubber

drawing pin

tape recorder

pen

ruler

notebook

desk

video recorder

computer

OHP

C Useful verbs

A maths teacher **teaches** maths. Her students **study** maths.

After school, students **do homework**.

At primary school, children **learn** to read and write.

A university teacher **gives a lecture on** chemistry and the students **take notes**.

Students can **do an** (**English**) **course** in many colleges and schools. At the end of a course, you often have to **take/do an exam**. You hope to **pass your exams**. You don't want to **fail your exams**.

If you pass your final exams at university, you **get a degree**.

Exercises

48.1 Match the subject on the left with the topic on the right.

1	maths	a	animals
2	physics	b	gymnastics
3	history	c	$25y + 32x = 51z$
4	geography	d	$e = mc^2$
5	physical education	e	H_2O
6	English	f	the countries of the world
7	chemistry	g	the 15th century
8	biology	h	computers
9	information technology	i	spelling

48.2 Look at the subjects in A. Which were your favourite subjects? Which did you not like?

48.3 Look at the picture for 30 seconds. Then cover it. How many of the ten objects can you remember? Write them down in English.

48.4 Which of the things in B opposite have you got in the room where you study English? Write down the words for everything you can see.

48.5 Choose a verb from C opposite to fill the gaps below. Put the verb in the correct form.

John did well at school. He always found it easy to (1) _____learn_____ and he always (2) _____ his homework. He (3) _____ all his school exams. Now he (4) _____ geography at university. He is also (5) _____ a special geology course. He enjoys sitting in lectures, listening to the lecturer and (6) _____ notes. He will (7) _____ his final exams next year. If he (8) _____, he will (9) _____ a degree in geography. If he (10) _____, he will be very sad. He would like to become a geography lecturer. He would like to (11) _____ lectures.

48.6 Choose the ten words from the opposite page which you most want to learn. Write them down in one column on a piece of paper and in a second column put a drawing (or a translation or a definition). Cover the words in the first column and look at the second column. Can you remember the words?

49 Communications

A Letters

date

15/7/98

letter

Dear Jane,

how are you? I hope
how is you

address

Martin Smith
46 Falcon Avenue
Banbury
Oxfordshire
OX16 9QT

post box

stamp

envelope

Don't forget to put a **stamp**
   on the **envelope**.
Don't forget to **post** the letters.

B Telephone and fax

answerphone   mobile phone   **(tele)phone**   phone box

Juan **makes** a lot of **phone calls**. He phones his girl friend every day.

Jill **sent** me a **fax** yesterday.

What is your **phone/fax number**?
330718 (= double three oh seven one eight)

C A typical phone conversation

SUE: Two three four six five oh.
NICK: Hello. It's Nick here. Can I speak to John, please.
SUE: I'm sorry, he isn't here at the moment. Can I take a message?
NICK: Thanks. Could you just tell him Nick called. I'll call back later.
SUE: OK. I'll tell him. Goodbye.
NICK: Bye.

D E-mail

computer   screen   keyboard   mouse   disk

Anne gets a lot of **e-mails** from New York.

What is your **e-mail address**?
Mollflanders@cup.cam.ac.uk (= Moll Flanders at C-U-P dot C-A-M dot A-C dot U-K)

> **Tip:** If possible, get an example of a letter and an e-mail in English. Write down any useful words or phrases in them.

Exercises

49.1 Have you got any of the things on the opposite page? Make a list. *answerphone*

49.2 What are the names of these things?

1 .....*keyboard*.....   4 ....   7 ....

2 ....   5 ....   8 ....

3 ....   6 ....   9 ....

49.3 Complete this phone conversation.

SALLY: 333091
MEENA: Hello. (1)................. Meena here. Can I (2)................. to Amal, please.
SALLY: I'm (3)................., he's at work (4)................. the moment.
        Can I (5)................. a message?
MEENA: It's all right. I'll (6)................. back later.
SALLY: OK, then. Bye.
MEENA: Bye.

49.4 Write down these numbers and addresses then read them aloud.

1 Two telephone or fax numbers that are important to you.
2 Two e-mail addresses that are important to you.

Now practise reading aloud the examples in the key at the end of the book.

49.5 Answer these questions.

1 Which is quickest – a phone call, a fax, an e-mail or a letter? *a phone call*
2 Which is cheapest – a phone call, a fax, an e-mail or a letter?
3 Have you sent all of these – a letter, a fax and an e-mail ? Have you received all of them?
4 Which is your favourite way of communicating with a friend?
5 Which is your favourite way of business communication?

50 Holidays

A Holiday (noun)

We **had a** wonderful **holiday** in Egypt in 1996.
I'm not working next week. I'**m on holiday**.
Are you **going on holiday** this summer?

B Types of holidays

We are going on **a package holiday** to Hong Kong. (everything is included, flights, hotel, etc.)
We're going to have a **winter holiday** this year. (often means skiing / winter sports)
I want to **go camping** this year. (sleep in a tent)
I'm going on a **walking holiday** in the Alps. (usually means walking up mountains)
A **coach tour** is a cheap way to go on holiday. (going in a big, comfortable bus)

C Transport

Are you **flying** to France from England?
No, we're going **by ferry**. (ship where you can take your car with you)
We're going **by car / by train / by bus**.
(See Units 14 and 41.)

D Don't forget to take with you ...

your **passport** (if you are going to another country)
a **visa** (a special stamp in your passport to go to some countries)
your **tickets**
some **traveller's cheques** and **currency** (money of the country you are going to)
a **camera**
a **phrase book** (if it's a different language)
your **luggage** /ˈlʌɡɪdʒ/

E When you are there ...

Send some **postcards**.
Try the **local food**.
Enjoy the **nightlife**. (discos, clubs, etc.)
Try to **speak the language**.
Go to the **Tourist Information Office** if you have any questions. (*or* the **Tourist Office**)

Exercises

50.1 Fill the gaps.

1 A: Are you working on Monday?
   B: No, I'm .... holiday.

2 A: Are you going .... holiday this year?
   B: Yes, I'm going camping.

3 A: Did you have a good .... in Greece?
   B: Yes, it was wonderful.

4 A: Are you flying to Italy?
   B: No, I'm going .... train.

50.2 These people are talking about their holidays. What type of holiday did they have?

1 Everything was included, meals, hotels, flights.
2 We were on the same coach for seven days. I was very tired.
3 We walked about 20 kilometres every day.
4 It wasn't very good. There wasn't much snow.

50.3 Put a plus (+) in the boxes for the different ways of travelling. Put one plus (+) for *sometimes true*, two for *very true* (++), three for *absolutely true!* (+++)

	you can take a lot of luggage	very fast	usually cheap	you see a lot as you travel	you can relax
ferry					
car					
flight					

50.4 Write the names of these things you need for a holiday.

1 ....   3 ....   5 ....

2 ....   4 ....   6 ....

50.5 What do we call:

1 Cheques you can use in different countries? t..................... c.....................
2 A special stamp or paper for your passport to enter a country? a v.....................

50.6 Fill the gaps in these sentences.

1 Don't forget to send me ..a postcard....
2 The .... is good; the discos are open all night.
3 I didn't try the .... food. I had hamburgers every day!
4 Is there a .... Office here? I want some information.
5 I'd like to go to Estonia for my holiday but I can't speak the ....

51 Shops and shopping

A Kinds of shops

butcher *

supermarket

book shop

toy shop

post office

hairdresser *

baker *

chemist *

newsagent *

gift shop

* These words are also for people's jobs. We often add 's and say: I'm going to the newsagent's to get a paper. Do you want anything from the butcher's?

B Department store

A department store is a large shop which sells a lot of different things – clothes, cosmetics, toys and so on.

H E R O D S		
• **BASEMENT** food, sports equipment	• **FIRST FLOOR** ladieswear	• **THIRD FLOOR** electrical goods, furniture
• **GROUND FLOOR** cosmetics, shoes, stationery	• **SECOND FLOOR** childrenswear, menswear, toys	• **FOURTH FLOOR** restaurant

(cosmetics = beauty products; stationery = pens, pencils, paper, etc.)

C Going shopping

You buy something from a **shop assistant**.
You pay for it at the **cash desk / till**.
You get a **receipt**. /rɪˈsiːt/

coins/change

cash

cheque book

credit card

D Useful phrases

Can I help you?
How much does this **cost**?
Can I pay by **cheque / credit card**?
No, **cash** only.
Sorry, I only have a £20 **note**; I don't have any **change** (coins).
Can I **try it on**?
Have you got a **bigger / smaller size / a different colour**?
Would you like a (**carrier**) **bag**?

Exercises

51.1 Match the item with the shop.

| toy shop | butcher's | baker's | gift shop | chemist's | newsagent's |

1 aspirin   3 sausages   5 souvenir T-shirt

2 beach ball   4 postcards   6 bread

51.2 Where do you need to go?

1 I want to get a newspaper. *The newsagent's.*
2 Your hair is too long.
3 I need some stamps.
4 We must get Jim a present.
5 I'd like to buy a book.
6 I want to buy everything in one shop.

51.3 Look at the department store plan in B. Which floor will you go to if you want to buy:

1 an armchair?   5 a skirt?   9 a tie?
2 lipstick?   6 some tennis balls?   10 a TV?
3 a cup of tea?   7 a pair of boots?   11 pens?
4 a packet of tea?   8 some baby clothes?   12 a doll?

51.4 Write the words for these definitions.

1 a person who sells things in a shop *shop assistant*
2 money not a cheque or credit card
3 a person who cuts hair
4 'plastic money'
5 a floor lower than the ground floor

Now write definitions in English for:

6 a £5 note   8 a receipt
7 the first floor   9 a cash desk

51.5 Make a list of ...

1 the shops in a street near you.
2 the departments there are in your favourite department store.

51.6 Fill the gaps in the dialogue.

CUSTOMER: How much does this shirt ....?
SHOP ASSISTANT: £25.
CUSTOMER: I'll take it, please. Can I .... by credit card?
SHOP ASSISTANT: Certainly.
I'll put your receipt in the ....

52 In a hotel

A At reception

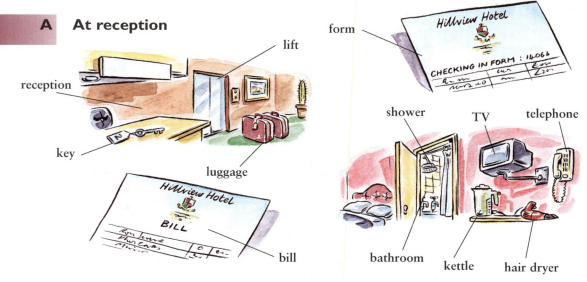

Do you have a **single room** (= for one person) a **double room** (= for two people)? How much is a single room with a bathroom?
I have a **reservation**. (= I booked a room) My name is …

The receptionist may say:
Your room is on the **first floor**. The **lift** is over there.
Here is your **key**.
Would you like some help with your **luggage**?
Can you **fill in** this **form**, please?
Sign here, please. (= write your name)
Please, **check** your bill. (= make sure it is correct)

When you leave you say,
Can I **check out**, please?
Can I have the **bill**, please?

B Using the telephone

How do I get an **outside line**? (You want to phone someone who is not in the hotel.)
What is the **code** for Korea / Poland, etc.?

Can I have **breakfast in my room**, please?
Can I have a **morning call**, please? At 6.30. (You want to wake up at 6.30.)
What time is breakfast/lunch/dinner?

C Changing money

You can often change money in a big hotel. Here are some useful phrases.
Can I (**ex**)**change** some money, please?
Can I **change** some dollars **into** pounds, please?
How many yen **to the** pound at the moment? (yen = Japanese **currency**)
Can I **cash** a traveller's cheque?

Exercises

52.1 Look at the pictures and complete the dialogue with words from the opposite page.

CLIENT: Can I have a [picture] (1)............. room for tonight, please?

RECEPTIONIST: Would you like a room with a [picture] (2)............. ?

CLIENT: Yes, please. And with a [picture] (3)............. , please.

RECEPTIONIST: All our rooms have a TV, a [picture] (4).............and a

[picture] (5)............. I can give you room 25. It has a view of

the [picture] (6)............. Here is your [picture] (7)............. .

The [picture] (8)............. is over there. It's on the second floor.

52.2 Match what you want on the left with what you need on the right.

You want:
1 to have a cup of tea in your room
2 to go to the top floor
3 to open your door
4 to get up at 6 a.m.
5 to phone your country
6 to watch the news
7 to wash your hair
8 to dry your hair

You need:
a the lift
b an outside line
c a shower
d a kettle
e a hair dryer
f a morning call
g a TV
h a key

52.3 Do you know?

1 How much does a hotel room cost in the capital of your country?
2 What is the code for Britain if you phone from your country?
3 How many US dollars are there to your own currency at the moment?
4 How much of your own currency is there to the pound?
5 Why are traveller's cheques useful when you are travelling?

52.4 You are on holiday in London with two other people. You want rooms for one night. Write a dialogue.

52.5 Write down six questions that you can ask in a hotel beginning: *Can I ...?*

53 Eating out

A **Places where you can eat**

café: you can have a cup of tea/coffee and a **snack** there (= something small to eat like a sandwich or a cake). They sometimes serve meals there too.

restaurant: you go there for a full meal; more expensive than a café.

bar/pub: bars and pubs serve alcohol and **soft drinks** (= non-alcoholic drinks like fruit juice and lemonade); you can usually have a meal or a snack there too.

sandwich bar: a place that serves lots of different kinds of sandwiches. People usually buy sandwiches and take them to eat in a different place, at work or in the park.

fast food restaurant: you can get a quick hot meal there, for example burger and chips.

self-service restaurant/café: you take what you want, pay for it and carry it to your table.

B **In a restaurant**

STARTERS	MAIN COURSE	DESSERT
• Tomato soup	• Roast beef, green peas, carrots and roast potatoes	• Ice-cream
• Melon	• Chicken salad	• Strawberries and cream
• Orange juice	• Steak, mashed potatoes and mixed vegetables	• Fruit salad
	• Fish, chips and beans	• Chocolate gateau
	• Cheese, ham or plain omelette	

C **Ordering food**

WAITER: Are you ready to order?

CUSTOMER: Yes, I'd like tomato soup and steak, please.

WAITER: Would you like the steak with chips or new potatoes? And how would you like your steak – rare, medium or well-done?

CUSTOMER: Well-done, please. And with chips.

WAITER: And what would you like to drink?

(*later*)

WAITER: Is everything all right?

CUSTOMER: Thank you, it's very nice.

Exercises

53.1 Which of the places in A opposite would you go to if you ...

1 want to buy something in the morning to eat at lunch-time at work? *a sandwich bar*
2 want a romantic dinner for two?
3 have three small children with you?
4 arrive half an hour early to meet a friend?
5 are very thirsty?

53.2 Do you have all the places in A in your country? Write down all the places you have. Give an example of an eating place of this type. *fast food restaurant — McDonald's*

53.3 Look at the menu on the opposite page.

1 What would you eat from the menu opposite?
2 What would a vegetarian eat? (Vegetarians don't eat meat.)

53.4 Choose one of the words in the box which can go with each of the words in each group.

steak   omelette   potatoes   gateau   ~~soup~~   salad

1 You can have tomato / vegetable / chicken .... *soup* .... to start.
2 Would you like a cheese / ham / plain ....?
3 I'll have the chicken / ham / fruit ....
4 I'd like some roast / mashed / new ....
5 Can I have the chocolate / strawberry / apricot ...., please.
6 Do you like your .... well-done / medium / rare?

53.5 There are some mistakes in this dialogue. Correct the mistakes.

WAITER: Are you ready for order?
CUSTOMER: Yes. I like vegetable soup and steak, please.
WAITER: What would you like your steak? Rare, medium or done good?
CUSTOMER: Rare, please.
WAITER: What you would like to drink?
CUSTOMER: A orange juice, please.

53.6 Cover the page opposite and write down all the words you can remember.
Then look at the page again and write down any words you forgot.

> **Tip:** Sometimes restaurants in other countries have English menus for tourists. Look at one of these. Write down any useful words you find.

54 Sports

A Ball games

We **play** all these sports. I **play** rugby. Do you **play** baseball?

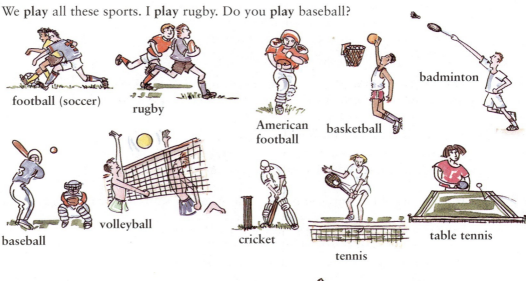

football (soccer) rugby

American football basketball

badminton

baseball volleyball cricket tennis table tennis

B Other popular sports

swimming running sailing motor racing

horse racing judo/karate skiing canoeing

We use **go** or **do** with most of these sports. I **go** running. He **does** canoeing.
We use **do** only with judo and karate. She **does** judo. I **do** karate.

C Asking questions about sports

Do you do any sports? Yes, **I go** swimming/running/sailing/canoeing.
Do you play football/tennis/badminton?
What's your favourite sport? I **like** motor racing **best**.
(See Unit 4.)

D Where we do sports

We play tennis/badminton/volleyball/basketball on a
   tennis/badminton/volleyball/basketball court.
We play football/cricket/rugby on a **football/cricket/rugby field** or **pitch**. We swim in a
   swimming pool.

Exercises

54.1 Cover the left-hand page and try to remember the names of these sports.

1 .... 3 .... 5 ....

2 .... 4 .... 6 ....

54.2 What sports do you think of when you see ...?

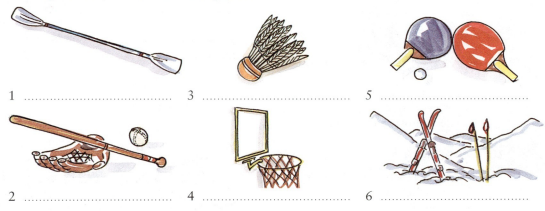

1 .... 3 .... 5 ....

2 .... 4 .... 6 ....

54.3 Ask questions for these answers.

1 _What's your favourite sport?_
   I like running best.
2 Do you ....?
   Yes, but not soccer, only American football.
3 ....?
   No, I don't do any at all. I prefer watching TV.
4 Do you ....?
   Yes. I go to the swimming pool every Friday.

54.4 Write the names of the sports you have done. Which ones do you like? Which do you not like? Which ones would you like to do?

> **Tip:** Make a page in your vocabulary book for 'sports'. Look at the sports pages of an English language newspaper. Write down the names of sports you do not know. Look them up in a dictionary.

55 Cinema

A Types of films

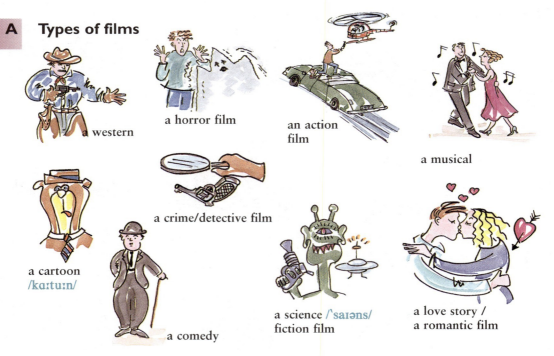

a western

a horror film

an action film

a musical

a cartoon /ˈkɑːtuːn/

a comedy

a crime/detective film

a science /ˈsaɪəns/ fiction film

a love story / a romantic film

Do you like **westerns**? No, I like **science fiction films** best.
The best **action film** I've seen was *Goldfinger* with James Bond.
If I see a **horror film**, I can't sleep.

B People in films

Zelda Glitzberg is a **film star**.
She lives in Hollywood.
She is **in** the new James Bond film.

Sean Connery **played** James Bond in *From Russia with Love*.

I like films by Italian **directors**.

C Watching films

Do you **go to the cinema** often?
Yes, I go every week.
No, I **watch videos** at home.

What's on at the cinema this week?
It's a comedy called *Airplane*.

Have you **seen** *The English Patient*?
Yes I saw it **on TV**.

Did you like *Dirty Harry*?
Yes, I **loved it / enjoyed it**.
No, it was **boring**. (= makes you want to fall asleep)

Exercises

55.1 **What types of films are these?**

1 Some cowboys rob a train. *western*
2 A flying saucer lands from Mars.
3 A dead person comes back to life.
4 James Bond saves the world.
5 Mickey Mouse goes on a picnic.
6 A man falls in love with his teacher.
7 A dead body is found in the river.
8 There are lots of songs and dancing.

55.2 **Word puzzle. How many words for other types of films can you make with the letters of ROMANTIC?**

```
        C  R  I  M  E
        _  O  _  _  _  R
     C  _  M  _  _  Y
        A  _  T  _  _  N
  S  _  _  _  N  C  _  F  _  _  _  _  _  N
     W  _  _  T  _  _  N
     M  _  _  I  C  _  L
        C  A  _  _  O  O  _
```

55.3 **Fill the gaps in these sentences.**

1 Do you prefer to go .... cinema or to watch TV?
2 We .... a video last night.
3 Who .... James Bond in *You Only Live Twice*?
4 Was Clint Eastwood .... *Dirty Harry*?
5 All the big .... live in Hollywood.
6 Stephen Spielberg is a famous American film ....

55.4 **Answer these questions for *yourself*.**

1 Name one science fiction film you have seen.
2 Who is your favourite film star?
3 Do you like detective films? Can you name one?
4 Can you watch horror films?

55.5 **Write down the English names of three films you have seen this year. You can learn vocabulary by remembering the English names of films. For example:**

Four Weddings and a Funeral
Mars Attacks!
Home Alone

55.6 **Try to name one example of each type of film from the opposite page!**

56 Leisure at home

A TV, radio, music, video

I **watch** TV every evening. [NOT I ~~see~~ TV.]
Did you **watch/see** the film about President Kennedy?
I **listen to** the radio every morning. [NOT I ~~hear~~ the radio.]
What **programmes** do you like best on TV and radio?
I like **watching** films on TV. (*or* I like to watch …)
I like **listening to** music on the radio. (*or* I like to listen …)
I often **listen to CDs** or **tapes** when I am relaxing.
At the weekend, we usually **watch a video**.

B Hobbies/activities at home

A lot of young people **play computer games** every day.
Do you use **the Internet**?
I really like **cooking**.
Do you like **gardening**? /ˈgɑːdnɪŋ/
We **grow flowers** and **vegetables** in our garden.
I live in a flat. I don't have **a garden**,
    but I have a lot of **house plants**.

C Reading

I **read** a lot at home.
What do you read?
I read **novels**. (= long stories)
I like **books about** nature/different countries, etc.
I like **magazines about** rock music and sport.
Do you read a **newspaper** every day?

D Time with other people

Sometimes we **invite friends around/have friends around**.
    (= we ask them to come to our house/flat)
I often **have people/have friends to dinner**.
My best friend **comes to stay** sometimes.
    (= sleeps in my house/flat)
I **talk to** my friends **on the phone** every evening. *or*
I **ring** my friends every evening.

E Just relaxing

Sometimes, I just **do nothing**.
I like to **have a sleep** after lunch.

Exercises

56.1 What are these people doing?

1 She's ....

4 She's ....

2 He's ....

5 She's using the ....

3 He's .... a ....

6 He's .... to a ....

56.2 Fill in the missing verbs.

1 Sometimes I ...*listen*..... to CDs or tapes.
2 I prefer to .... magazines more than newspapers.
3 I .... to my sister on the phone every Sunday.
4 A lot of people like to .... a sleep after lunch.
5 Do you ever .... friends to dinner?
6 The children .... computer games every evening.
7 Shall we .... a video tonight?
8 Did you .... the programme about Namibia yesterday?
9 My father .... vegetables in his garden.

56.3 Answer for *yourself*.

1 If you have friends around, what do you like to do?
2 Does anyone come to stay at your house/flat?
3 What do you like to read most?
4 How often do you ring your friends?

56.4 Interesting or boring? Put these leisure activities in order, from *most interesting* to *most boring*, in your opinion.

> gardening   cooking   reading   using the Internet   watching videos
> listening to music   doing nothing

most interesting   *most boring*

57 Crime

A Crimes, people who do them, and verbs

crime	robbery	murder /ˈmɜːdə/	burglary /ˈbɜːglərɪ/	mugging
person	a robber	a murderer	a burglar	a mugger
verb	to rob somebody or a place (e.g. a bank)	to murder somebody	to break into a house/flat (break/broke/broken)	to mug somebody

crime	car theft	drug pushing/ dealing	terrorism	shoplifting
person	a car thief /θiːf/	a drug pusher/ dealer	a terrorist	a shoplifter
verb	to steal a car (steal/stole/stolen)	to sell drugs (sell/sold/sold)	to attack somebody or a place	to steal things from a shop

There was **a burglary** at the school last night.
John West **murdered** his wife.
There are a lot of **muggings** in the city centre.

A robber **robs** a person or a place. That bank **was robbed** yesterday. My sister **was robbed** in the city centre.
A thief **steals** something (**steal/stole/stolen**). Somebody **stole** my bicycle. [NOT Somebody robbed my bicycle.]
I **was robbed** in the city centre yesterday. [NOT I was stolen.]

B The law /lɔː/

A student **was arrested for** shoplifting this morning.
The police came to the school and spoke to his teacher.
The student has to **go to court** next week.
If he is **guilty** he will have to **pay a fine**. /ˈgɪltɪ/
If he is **innocent** he can go home. /ˈɪnəsənt/
I don't think he will **go to prison**.

C Other crime problems

Some **vandals** broke the windows in the telephone box.
  (A vandal breaks and smashes things.)
We have a lot of **vandalism** in my town.
A lot of young people **take drugs** nowadays.
Is **football hooliganism** a problem in your country? /ˈhuːlɪgənɪzm/
  (A **football hooligan** is a person who goes to a football match and makes trouble.)

Exercises

57.1 **What do we call ...?**

1 a person who steals cars? *a car thief*
2 a person who kills someone?
3 a person who steals things from shops?
4 a person who robs people's houses and flats?
5 a person who attacks someone in the street and steals their money?
6 a person who sells dangerous drugs?

57.2 **Fill the gaps in these sentences.**

1 There were a lot of football h*ooligans*... near the stadium.
2 The police officer a..................... her for shoplifting.
3 Some v..................... destroyed all the flowers in the park.
4 He had to pay a f..................... of £50 for parking his car in the wrong place.
5 There are a lot of b..................... in this part of the city, so always close the windows.
6 The police made a mistake; she was i..................... She did not steal the money.
7 People who t..................... drugs often do other crimes too.
8 A group of t..................... have attacked the airport.
9 He murdered his wife. He was in p..................... for 20 years.

57.3 **What do you think should happen to these people? Choose from the list a – i on the right. If you do not like the list, what do you think should happen to them?**

1 A man murdered his wife and three children.
2 A student with no money stole a book from a bookshop.
3 A woman sold some drugs to a teenager.
4 Some terrorists attacked a bus and killed 5 people.
5 A woman parked her car and blocked the traffic.
6 A teenager broke some trees in the park.
7 A man who drank too much alcohol drove his car and crashed.

a fine of £100
b 30 years in prison
c six months in prison
d death
e five years in prison
f in prison for life
g a fine of £50
h must work in a hospital for six months
i must not drive a car for a year

57.4 **What do you think? Put all the crimes on the opposite page in a list, from *least serious* to *most serious*.**

57.5 **Choose five or six words opposite and use them to make your own sentences.**

58 The media

A Radio and TV programmes

The news *is* on TV at 6 o'clock every night. (= important things that happen) [NOT The news ~~are~~ on TV.]

Do you watch **soaps / soap operas**? *Home and Away* is my favourite. (Soap operas are stories about people's lives. They are often on TV every day.)

I like **nature programmes** best. (= programmes about animals, birds, etc.)

I watched **a documentary** last night about drugs and young people. (= programme looking at a social problem or question)

In **talk shows**, people talk about very personal and private things in their lives.

The children watch **cartoons** on Saturday mornings. (For example, Disney films with animals that talk.) (See Unit 55.)

I always watch **sport programmes** and **films**.

B Newspapers and magazines

In most countries there are **morning newspapers** and **evening newspapers**.

Every month, I buy a **magazine**.

My mother buys **women's magazines**.

I like **news magazines** like *Newsweek* and *Time*.

My little brother buys **comics**.

Other types of magazines: **sports magazines / computer magazines / teenage magazines** (See Unit 56.)

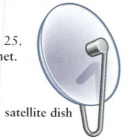

C Media and technology

Do you have **satellite TV**?

How many **channels** do you have? We have 25.

You can read some newspapers **on the Internet**.

satellite dish

computer

D People and the media

There was **an interview with** the US President on TV last night.

The **reporters** are outside Zelda Glitzberg's house. (= People who go out and get the news stories where they happen.)

My sister is **a journalist**; she writes for *The Oxford Times* newspaper. (= Person who writes articles.)

English Vocabulary in Use (elementary)

Exercises

58.1 Fill the gaps in these sentences.

1 The news ....is....... on Channel 3 at nine o'clock every night.
2 Ten million people watch this .... every week. It's very popular.
3 There was a .... about traffic problems in cities on TV last night.
4 I saw a .... programme about birds in Antarctica.
5 My sister is 13; she reads .... magazines every week. She likes the love stories.
6 With my computer I can get the sports news on the ....
7 Most young children don't read newspapers, they prefer ....

58.2 Match the left-hand column with the right-hand column. Draw lines.

1 Talking about family problems   a International news
2 Film of elephants in Africa   b Sports programme
3 Football cup final   c Soap opera
4 Reports from all over the world   d Nature programme
5 Maria decides not to marry Philip   e Talk show

58.3 What can we find in these magazines? Match the left-hand column with the right-hand column. Draw lines.

1 a computer magazine   a articles about health
2 a women's magazine   b pictures of pop music stars
3 a news magazine   c news about the Internet
4 a teenage magazine   d interviews with politicians

58.4 What do you call ...

1 a person who goes out and gets stories for newspapers? **A reporter**
2 a person who writes articles in newspapers and magazines?
3 a newspaper you can buy every day after about 5 p.m.?
4 a magazine that children read, with cartoon pictures?
5 a programme on TV about animals, birds, etc?

58.5 Answer these questions for *yourself*.

1 Do you read a morning or an evening newspaper?
2 How many TV channels do you have?
3 Is satellite TV popular in your country?
4 How many hours of TV do you watch every day?
5 What are your favourite kinds of TV programmes?

58.6 Write a paragraph about the media in your country. Use words from the opposite page.

59 Everyday problems

A At home

The TV **isn't working**. Can you **repair** it?

The washing machine is **broken**.   We need to **mend** it.

The plants **are dying**.
Did you forget to **water** them?

The room is **untidy**. We must **tidy** it.

I've lost my keys. Will you help me **look for** them?

You've **cut** your finger.
You should **put on a plaster**.

You've **had a row** /raʊ/ **with** a friend. Will you **apologise**? (= say 'I'm sorry'.)

B At work

Carla had a bad day at work yesterday. She was **late for** work.

She had **too much work to do**.

Her colleague was **in a bad mood**.

Her **computer crashed**.

The photocopier was **out of order**.

The coffee machine **wasn't working**.

Tip: When you need to make a list of things to do, make it in English, e.g.
    Mend my bike   Water the plants   Tidy my desk

Exercises

59.1 Look at the pictures. What is the problem?

1 Sam   The coffee machine isn't working.
2 Sarah ....
3 Maria ....
4 Tommy ....
5 Tina   ....
6 Ross   ....
7 Delia ....
8 Kim   ....

59.2 Write down three nouns that can go with these words:
1 broken   window/cup/glass ....   4 late for ....
2 cut   ....   5 a .... that isn't working
3 untidy ....   6 too much ....

59.3 Put the problems in two groups, *serious* or *not serious*.

1 a TV that doesn't work
2 dying plants
3 a cut finger
4 being late for work
5 a colleague in a bad mood
6 a photocopier that is out-of-order
7 a coffee machine that isn't working
8 a broken washing machine
9 an untidy bedroom
10 a row with a friend
11 a computer crash
12 lost keys
13 too much work

59.4 Look at Carla's problems in B. What could she do?

She was late for work — get a new alarm clock.

59.5 Can you think of three everyday problems that you, or people you know, have had recently? Write them down in English. Use a dictionary if you need one.

60 Global problems

A Natural disasters

There was a **hurricane / snowstorm / forest fire** there last year.
hurricane = when there is a very strong wind
snowstorm = when there is a lot of snow and wind at the same time
forest fire = when it is very dry and trees catch fire

San Francisco has had a lot of **earthquakes**. (= when the earth moves)
The river often **floods** after heavy rain. (= when there is too much water)

B Man-made problems

There are too many people in some places. Cities are too **crowded**.
Many people are:
poor = they do not have enough money
hungry = they do not have enough food
homeless = they do not have a place to live
unemployed = they do not have a job

There is a lot of **pollution** in many cities. (= when the air, water or earth is dirty and bad
   for people, plants and animals)
The **air pollution** is very bad today.
The river is **polluted** and a lot of fish have died.

The American **War** of Independence lasted eight years. (= fighting between two or more
   countries or nationalities)

The **traffic jams** in the city are terrible **in the rush hour**. (= times when everyone is going
   to work)

He had a **car crash** on the way to work.

There's a teachers' **strike** today. (= when they will not work)
The bus drivers are **on strike**.

Exercises

60.1 What problems can you see in the pictures?

1 ....strike...........

4 ....

7 ....

2 ....

5 ....

8 ....

3 ....

6 ....

9 ....

60.2 Write down the natural disasters in A and the names of places they have happened.

hurricane — Florida

60.3 Write down all the problems in B that you have in your country and the places where you have them.

poor people — small villages

60.4 Put all the words on the opposite page into groups in any way that seems appropriate to you. You may use as many groups as you wish.

hurricane, snowstorm, flood — problems because of the weather

60.5 Fill the gaps with a word from the opposite page.

1 Cars make air ....pollution............... worse in towns.
2 Their wages were very low so the workers went on ....
3 My great-grandfather died in the First World ....
4 Jack had a .... last year but fortunately no-one was hurt.
5 Japan often has .... and Siberia often has ....
6 When people are ...., they sometimes have to sleep on the streets.

> **Tip:** Try to listen to or watch the news in English every day.

Answer key

Unit 1

1.1
and 1.2   Check your work with a teacher if you are not sure about your answers.

1.3

noun	verb	adjective
book house word man	speak have write say	good new right blue

1.4   *Possible answers:*

to, for, with, below

1.5   2 question
3 phrase
4 sentence
5 question
6 sentence

1.6   1 books
2 man
3 No, it's a preposition.
4 No, it's a noun.
5 No, it's a sentence.
6 No, it's an adjective. The adverb is *badly*.

1.7   *Possible answers:*

2 black, green, blue, red
3 speak, English
4 It depends where you live.
5 make a mistake; do homework; have a shower

Unit 2

2.1   *Possible answers:*

have a party, a shower, lunch, a lesson, a cup of tea, a meeting, etc.

2.2 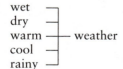 wet
dry
warm — weather
cool
rainy

2.3

name of family	words in family
education	school teacher exam student
weather	rain sun cloud snow ice

2.4 *Possible pictures:*

1   **a plane <u>lands</u>**   2   **sunny weather**   3   **under** the table

2.5 *Possible words:*

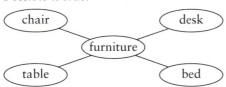 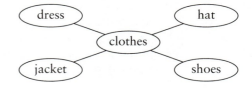

Unit 3

3.1 *Possible answers:*

1 coffee / tea / juice … toast / bread / fruit / an egg
2 an appointment
3 tennis / squash / rugby / darts / football / chess / cards
4 party
5 shower / bath / wash
6 exam
7 meeting
8 coffee / cup of tea / drink / sandwich
9 swim
10 dinner / supper / a meal / something to eat

3.2 *Possible answers:*

1 I've got one brother and two sisters.
2 I have them at 9.30 every day.
3 I have a sandwich and a cup of tea.
4 No, I have to go on Wednesday and Friday.
5 I've got two.
6 Yes, I always have a party.
7 I usually have pasta or fish.

3.3

Across	*Down*
1 meal	2 exam
3 party	4 tea
5 game	

3.4 *Possible answers:*

1 Why don't you have a drink / some water / a cup of tea?
2 Bye! Have a good time! *or* Have a good journey!
3 Oh! have you got a cold?
4 Is that new? Can I have a look?

Unit 4

4.1   2 Soraya and Mehmet are going shopping.
3 Imran is going to Cairo.
4 The Patels are going to the beach.
5 Natasha is going fishing.

4.2   2 We're going sightseeing today.
3 Jo went up to the top of the hill. *or* Jo went down to the bottom of the hill.
4 Let's go fishing today.
5 She went out of the shop.

4.3 *Possible answers:*

I sometimes go swimming.   I never go skiing.
I sometimes go dancing.   I never go fishing.
I always go sightseeing.

4.4 2 On Tuesday Alison is going to write to Juan.
3 On Wednesday she is going to watch the World Cup on TV.
4 On Thursday she is going to have a tennis lesson.
5 On Friday Alison is going to go to the cinema.

4.5 *Possible answers:*

From Cambridge, trains go to London, Norwich, Ely and Peterborough. Buses go to Oxford, to Heathrow and to Scotland from Cambridge. From Cambridge roads go to London, to the sea and to Huntingdon.

Unit 5

5.1 2 What is the woman doing? She's reading a book.
3 What are the girls doing? They are playing tennis.
4 What is the man in the house doing? He's washing-up. / He's doing the washing-up.
5 What is the dog doing? It's sleeping.
6 What is the man in the garden doing? He's gardening. / He's doing the gardening.

5.2 2 What does Lara Brown do? She's a secretary.
3 What does Sophie Hicks do? She's a doctor.
4 What do Ted and Joe do? They're students.

5.3 2 What did Lara Brown do? She went to a meeting.
3 What did Sophie Hicks do? She talked to five patients.
4 What did Ted and Jo do? They wrote an essay.

5.4 *Possible answers:*

I usually do the washing-up.
My husband usually does the washing.
My son has to do his homework every day.
My husband does his exercises every morning.
He does business with Eastern Europe.
I hate doing the housework.
I love doing the gardening.
I always do my best.

5.5 ANNA: Where did you go on your holidays? To London?
PAVEL: No, we didn't go to London this year. We went to Scotland.
ANNA: Does your grandmother live in Scotland?
PAVEL: No, she doesn't but my uncle does.

Unit 6

6.1 1 make   3 do   5 make
2 do   4 do/take; do/take

6.2 1 made/makes me (feel) sad
2 make me (feel) tired
3 made me (feel) angry

6.3 1 He's making a photocopy.   3 The children are making a noise.
         2 She's making tea.   4 They're making a video / a film.

6.4 1 Can I take a photo of you?
         2 He's 25 but he never does his own washing. He takes his dirty clothes to his mother's.
         3 What do you think, yes or no? We must make a decision today.
         4 I have to make an appointment with the doctor. Do you have her phone number?
         5 I make mistakes when I speak English.
         6 Are you doing/taking an exam tomorrow?

Unit 7

7.1 2 back home   4 from   6 out of / back from
         3 into   5 see

7.2 *Possible answers:*

         1 I usually come home at five-thirty.
         2 I'm from / I come from Scotland/Jamaica/Pakistan/Latvia/Bolivia, etc.
         3 I sit down and talk to my friends / take out my books.

7.3 1 Come in!
         2 Come here, please!
         3 to come along?

7.4 1 come   2 came   3 comes   4 Are … coming

7.5 *Possible meanings and sentences:*

         1 **come round** can mean 'come to someone's house/flat'.
            Do you want to come round this afternoon for a coffee?
         2 **come across** can mean 'meet/find for the first time'.
            I come across lots of new words when I read English books.
         3 **come up** can mean 'be mentioned / occur in conversation'.
            When new words come up in class, the teacher tells us the meaning.

Unit 8

8.1 *Possible answers:*

         1 takes, 10
         2 takes, an hour, Cambridge to London
         3 takes, an hour

8.2 1 take an exam.
         2 took some lessons. / took a course.
         3 take a course / take some lessons
         4 take your driving test.

8.3 1 takes the train.   3 takes the bus.
         2 can / could / have to / should take a taxi.   4 take the Underground.

8.4 1 a camera   3 my passport
         2 an umbrella   4 my books and pens/pencils

8.5 For some people, it takes them about an hour.

Unit 9

9.1   2 bring   4 Take   6 bring
            3 bring   5 take

9.2   1 take; bring ... back   2 brought ... back   3 take; bring ... back

9.3   1 Yesterday he brought me some flowers.
            2 You must take your passport when you travel.
            3 Come to my house and bring your guitar.
            4 Go to the secretary and take these papers, please.
            5 Everybody is going to bring food to the party.

9.4   1 brought   2 brought   3 took   4 taken ... bring

Unit 10

10.1   *Possible answers:*

        1 tired   2 sick   3 hot

10.2   2 gets light.   4 'm getting wet
          3 's getting better.   5 'm getting cold.

10.3   2 a doctor   5 a newspaper
          3 a glass   6 a taxi / a bus / a train
          4 a pen/pencil and paper   7 a job

10.4   1 gets to   2 gets to   3 can I get to

10.5   *Possible answers:*

        1 In Britain, people get married mostly when they are 20 to 30 years old.
        2 People usually get married at the weekend, mostly on Saturday. April, May and June are very
           popular months (spring and summer).
        3 I get home at about 5 o'clock. I get there by car.
        4 get

Unit 11

11.1   1 c   2 d   3 g   4 f   5 b   6 h   7 e   8 a

11.2   1 on   3 on; up   5 off   7 on
          2 off   4 off   6 on with   8 on

11.3   2 Someone is doing up a shoe.
          3 A plane is taking off.
          4 Someone is turning on the oven.

11.4 *Possible answers:*

There are lots of different ways to answer this question. This is one way.

Words connected with dressing and daily routine
do up (e.g. coat)
put something on
take off (e.g. shoes)
get up

Words connected with movement
come on
take off (aeroplane)

Words connected with equipment
turn up
turn down (stereo)
turn on
turn off
go off

Words connected with people or things doing well or getting better
get on
get over

Words connected with people speaking
turn down (an offer)
go on

11.5   1   took off   3   went on
         2   took off   4   got over

Unit 12

12.1 *Possible answers:*

1   seven o'clock.
2   a shower.
3   tea and toast
4   car.
5   eleven

12.2   2   washes her clothes every Saturday.
         3   cleans the house every weekend.
         4   watches TV (*or* television) every evening.
         5   goes for a walk every Sunday.

12.3 *Possible questions:*

2   often do you go for a walk?
3   do you go to work?
4   do you have dinner?

Unit 13

13.1   2   told   4   tell; said   6   said
         3   said   5   said

13.2
1 you tell me where the railway station is
2 do you say 'tree' in German
3 tell me the time
4 say goodbye (to you)
5 tell me when the exam is
6 answer the phone, please

13.3 *Possible answers:*

1 Say Happy New Year   5 Tell a joke
2 Answer the door   6 Talk to a friend
3 Ask for the bill   7 Ask someone to help you
4 Reply to a letter

We can also say 'answer a letter', but not 'reply to the door'!

13.4
1 Ask for the bill in Spanish.
2 Ask how much something is in Malay.
3 Say Merry Christmas in Swedish.
4 Say good morning in Japanese.
5 Say thank you in Arabic.

Unit 14

14.1   2 danced   4 run   6 fell   8 walk
        3 swims   5 climbing   7 jumped; swam

14.2   1 ride   3 takes   5 take; go by   7 ride
        2 drives   4 drives   6 ride   8 take

Note you can also use *go by* with all these forms of transport (but without 'the' or 'a')
i.e. you can go to work by bicycle, go home by underground/taxi, etc.

14.3 *Possible answers:*

2 I ride my bike once a week.   5 I drive my car every day.
3 I swim in the sea once a year.   6 I go dancing once a month.
   I swim in a pool once a week.   7 I go climbing once a year.
4 I never jog.

14.4 *Possible answers:*

Please pass the salt.   Please pass the water.
Please pass the pepper.   Please pass the salad.
Please pass the bread.   Please pass the sauce.

14.5
2 Maria drove her grandmother to the city yesterday.
3 Bill caught the 9.45 train to London yesterday.
4 I took a taxi home from the station yesterday.
5 Jane fell when she rode her bike yesterday.

Unit 15

15.1   1 because   3 before   5 although
        2 and   4 so   6 if

15.2 *Possible sentences:*

Mary agreed to marry Paul after they decided to set up a business together.
Mary will marry Paul although/though she doesn't love him.
Mary agreed to marry Paul and they had two sons.
Mary agreed to marry Paul because he was a pop star.
Mary will marry Paul before he moves to London.
Mary will marry Paul but she doesn't love him.
Mary agreed to marry Paul if he moved to London.
Mary agreed to marry Paul so he moved to London.
Mary will marry Paul when he moves to London.

15.3 Check with a teacher or a dictionary if you are not sure if your answers are correct or not.

15.4
1 as well / too / also	3 like	5 than
2 Even	4 Only	

15.5 *Possible answers:*

I only play tennis in the summer.
It is too cold to swim here even in summer.
She plays the piano better than I do.
He swims like a fish.
I like listening to music and I like reading also.
I like going skiing too.
I often go skiing with the children and sometimes my husband comes as well.

15.6 *Possible answers:*

1 I enjoy it.
2 I do all the exercises in this book.
3 I am also studying Spanish.
4 it is very difficult.
5 I was fifteen.
6 I can manage in British hotels.
7 not this year.

Unit 16

16.1 1 an hour   2 a century   3 a week   4 a year

16.3 September
April, June and November
thirty one
February
twenty nine

This is a traditional rhyme which people use to help them remember the number of days of the month. It means that:
September, April, June and November have 30 days. The other months have 31 days except for February which has 28 days and 29 days in a leap year.

16.4
1 Monday	5 Wednesday	9 February
2 August	6 January	10 September
3 October	7 April	11 Tuesday
4 Saturday	8 Thursday	12 November

16.5 1 T F S (first letters of the days of the week)
2 A S O N D (first letters of the months)
3 A W (first letters of the four seasons)

16.6 I'm going to a party on <u>S</u>aturday for Jill's birthday. Her birthday is on <u>T</u>hursday but she wanted to have the party on a <u>w</u>eekend. She's having a barbecue. I think June is a good month to have a birthday because of the weather. I love going to barbecues <u>in</u> the summer. My birthday is in the <u>w</u>inter and it's too cold to eat outside.

16.7 *Possible answers:*

It is only possible here to give answers to some of these questions. Check with your teacher if you are not sure if your answers to any of the other questions are correct or not.
1 900   6 Thirty
2 Tuesday or Wednesday   9 July

Unit 17

17.1 1 In   2 for   3 from   4 to   5 At   6 for

17.2
the 19th century }
the 18th century }   the past

the 20th century *   the present

the 21st century * }
the 22nd century }   the future

* If you are using this book after the year 2000, then *the twentieth century* is the past and not *the present* and *the twenty first century* is *the present* and not *the future*.

17.3 1 Probably tomorrow.   2 Probably a week ago.   3 In a few minutes.

17.4 *Possible answers:*

2 I sometimes go to school by bus. I normally go by car.
3 I never play football.
4 I often watch TV.
5 I occasionally drink milk. I usually drink coffee.
6 I never wear a hat.
7 I often eat chocolate.
8 I sometimes go to bed at 10. I usually go to bed at 11.
9 I sometimes go to the theatre.

17.5 John plays tennis twice a week. He practises the piano once a week and he has a business meeting in Germany once a month.

Sally and Amy play tennis three times a week. They practise the piano twice a day. They go to Germany for a business meeting six times a year. *or* They have a business meeting in Germany six times a year.

17.6 *Possible answer:*

I usually get up early. I always have a cup of coffee when I wake up. I often work at home but sometimes I go to a school to teach. I never drive. Sometimes I walk to school and sometimes I go by bus. Now and then I have lunch in a park near school; but I hardly ever have a hot lunch. I normally eat a sandwich and occasionally I have an apple as well. Once a week I visit a friend and we go to the cinema together or have a meal in a restaurant.

Unit 18

18.1 1 here   2 here   3 there   4 there

18.2 1 back from Paris.   2 everywhere.

18.3 The top of the tree.

The middle of the tree.

The bottom of the tree.

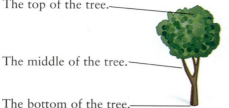

The back of the bus.

The side of the bus.

The front of the bus.

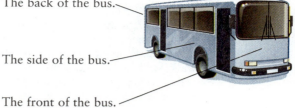

18.4 *Possible answers:*

1 When I studied English, I studied at home, in Britain.
2 Yes, I'm going to Dublin and to the USA.
3 At the moment I have a pen in my right hand.
4 The answer key.
5 The unit on **Have** is at the beginning of this book (Unit 3). Note *at*.
6 The unit on **Feelings** is in the middle of this book (Unit 34). Note *in*.

18.5 1 abroad   2 out   3 away   4 away; abroad

Unit 19

19.1 2 badly   4 fast [NOT ~~fastly~~]   6 well
3 loudly   5 quietly

19.2 *Possible answers:*

1 Usually, a quiet person is better.   4 A right answer is best in class!
2 Most people like a fast bus.   5 To speak politely – always.
3 A friendly person!   6 Usually it's better to speak in a normal way.

19.3

```
w  r  o  n  g  o
e  c  i  b  a  d
l  u  b  g  e  z
l  o  u  d  h  i
s  e  f  a  s  t
```

19.4

word	definition	right (✓)	wrong (✗)
suddenly	very slowly		✗
sadly	in an unhappy way	✓	
strangely	not in a normal way	✓	
quickly	very slowly		✗
easily	with no difficulty	✓	

Suddenly means very quickly, when you are not expecting it.
Quickly is similar to 'fast' when fast is an adverb, not when it is an adjective.

Unit 20

20.2   2 give, gave, given; take, took, taken
         3 come, came, come; go, went, gone
         4 make, made, made; break, broke, broken
         5 walk, walked, walked; run, ran, run
         6 wake, woke, woken; sleep, slept, slept
         7 remember, remembered, remembered; forget, forgot, forgotten
         8 rise, rose, risen; fall, fell, fell
         9 win, won, won; lose, lost, lost
       10 buy, bought, bought; sell, sold, sold

20.3

1 woke/got	4 drove	7 ran	10 made	13 went
2 ate	5 read	8 bought	11 left	14 slept
3 drank	6 wrote	9 sat	12 met	

20.4

1 swum	3 spent	5 caught
2 stolen	4 become	6 hurt; broken

20.5 *Possible sentences:*

Bill brought me a present from the USA.
I chose a strawberry ice-cream.
Snow fell all day yesterday.
I felt very cold last night.
We flew to Paris last summer.
My little brother kept a pet mouse in his bedroom.
Jack paid for our meal.
Mary spoke good Spanish.
My brother taught me to play football.
I told him to help you.
I thought you were at home.
Manchester United won the game.

Unit 21

21.1

1 money	3 advice	5 work
2 milk; butter	4 air	6 traffic

21.2   1 heavy luggage   5 brown bread
         2 useful information   6 cold water
         3 bad news   7 space travel
         4 modern furniture

21.3 brown sugar; heavy traffic; good advice; expensive accommodation; fresh air; hard work; brown rice; delicious spaghetti; unsalted butter; cold milk; Indian tea; Colombian coffee

21.4

1 is/was	3 is/was	5 is/was
2 is/was	4 is; was	6 is/was

2 Where can I get some <u>information</u> about your country?
3 Let me give you <u>some</u> advice.
4 Cook <u>this</u> spaghetti for ten minutes.
5 Can I have <u>some</u> bread, please?
6 Mary is looking for a new <u>job</u>.
7 We should buy some new <u>furniture</u>.
8 The east of the country usually has better weather than the west.
9 We went on two long <u>journeys</u> last year.
10 I must find <u>some</u> new accommodation soon.

Unit 22

22.1 *Possible answers:*

2	terrible/horrible/awful/bad	5	awful/horrible
3	terrible/awful	6	wonderful/lovely
4	excellent/great/wonderful	7	bad

22.2 *Possible answers:*

1 Yes, it's very nice. / Yes it's lovely.
2 Oh, how awful!
3 That's an excellent idea. *or* Yes, great!
4 Yes, there's the *Ritz*. It's the best restaurant in town.
5 She/He's a wonderful person! (We hope you can say this!)

22.3 1 c   2 e   3 f   4 a   5 b   6 d

22.4

good (+)	bad (-)
gorgeous	dreadful
marvellous	ghastly
fine	horrendous
superb	
brilliant	

22.5

gorgeous boy/girl   ghastly man/restuarant
marvellous weather/food   horrendous traffic/person
fine weather/day
superb idea/view

Unit 23

23.1 1 wonderful/lovely

2 horrible

3 (very) kind of you

4 (very) naughty

23.2

1	stupid	3	lovely	5	nice	7 horrible
2	wonderful	4	difficult	6	easy-going	

23.3 Most people probably think they are most of these things at some time, or at least the positive ones!

23.4   2 of   3 to   4 of

Unit 24

24.1   1 John is waiting for a train to London.
2 This bicycle belongs to the hotel.
3 The children thanked their grandmother for the money.
4 Sally is listening to her walkman.
5 He apologised for his mistake.
6 Let me pay for our tickets.
7 Billy is thinking about the holidays.

24.2   *Possible answers:*

2 after people.	6 for a new one.
3 for them	7 forward to it.
4 forward to it.	8 after the children
5 at me	

24.3   1 to   2 at   3 to   4 in   5 to   6 of

24.4   3 Hiroshi wasn't used to eating British food.   5 He was used to expensive shops.
4 He was used to traffic jams.   6 He wasn't used to British money.

24.5   *Possible answers:*

1 I was good at languages and bad at physical education.
2 I usually ask for a black coffee.
3 I am proud of my family.
4 I am afraid of going to the dentist.
5 I like listening to folk music.
6 I am looking forward to my holiday.
7 I belong to a teachers' club.
8 I am used to eating lots of different kinds of food.

Unit 25

25.1   2 rewrite (*or* redo)   5 half-price
3 informal   6 unsafe
4 unhappy

25.2   *Possible answers:*

He and his two ex-wives are all good friends.
An ex-president is giving a lecture here tomorrow.
It is impossible to read his handwriting.
Pre-school children learn by playing.
This work is not very good. Please redo it.

25.3   2 nerves before an exam
3 a wrong answer, an answer that is not correct
4 a book that has not been read
5 to tell a story again
6 a brother with one parent the same (for example, perhaps with the same mother but not the same father)

7 a letter that is not finished
8 a drink with no alcohol in it (for example, fruit juice, cola)
9 to read a book for a second time
10 to send a letter to a new address (to forward a letter)

25.4 *Possible answers:*

non: a non-stick pan   pre: a pre-lunch drink
in: an incomplete answer   re: to repaint a room
im: an impolite question   un: an unanswered question

25.5 *Possible answer:*

This paragraph is a rather silly story but it uses most of the words in the table.

He is a very unhappy ex-president. He never sees his ex-wife or his pre-school grandchildren. He lives in a house which is a half-hour bus ride from the city centre in an unsafe area. It is very crowded there and it is impossible for non-residents to park there. He is rewriting his autobiography for the third time in a very informal style. I don't know why he redoes it so often. He is sure that the book will only sell if it is sold at half-price.

25.6 2 uncomfortable   4 informal   6 unhappy   8 incorrect
      3 unsafe   5 non-smoking   7 impolite

Unit 26

26.1 2 happily   3 instructor   4 word processor   5 swimmer   6 useful

26.2 *Possible answers:*

You may be able to think of some other possible combinations.

2 fast worker/car/swimmer
3 beautiful picture/beach/book/weather/smile
4 sandy beach
5 sunny weather/smile
6 hard worker
7 useful idea/book/car
8 endless beach/fun
9 useless idea/book (Note that you can also say I'm a useless swimmer. It is quite colloquial and means I am no good at swimming.)

26.3 1 politics   2 sociology   3 economics   4 psychology

26.4 Check with a teacher if you are not sure if your answers are right or not.

26.5 2 a person who travels   7 the opposite of doing something well
      3 the opposite of fast   8 a thing for opening tins
      4 with lots of hope   9 the study of maths
      5 weather when it is raining   10 a person who plays football
      6 it doesn't hurt

Unit 27

27.1 2 lose   4 cooker   6 quite   8 cook
      3 felt   5 fell   7 loose

27.2

word	sounds like?	yes (✓)	sounds like?	yes (✓)
lose	juice		shoes	✓
loose	juice	✓	shoes	
quite	right	✓	higher	
quiet	right		higher	✓

27.3　2　checks it.
　　　　3　borrow your camera?
　　　　4　afternoon.
　　　　5　wait for the bus.
　　　　6　lend me £1 for the phone?
　　　　7　quiet.

27.4　*Possible answers:*

　　　　1　I am expecting my brother at 5.30. (= He said he would come at 5.30)
　　　　2　I hope to learn a lot of new words. (= I really want to learn new words)
　　　　3　Sometimes I borrow books and tapes.
　　　　4　Yes, but only to my *best* friend!

Unit 28

28.1　*Possible answers:*

　　　　My mother was born in Hull on June 19 1907.
　　　　My father was born in South Africa on June 4 1909.
　　　　My brother was born in London on June 6 1940.
　　　　My husband was born in Russia on February 6 1946.
　　　　My son was born in Cambridge on October 16 1988.

28.2　2　Elvis Presley was born in 1935 and died in 1977.
　　　　3　Genghis Khan was born in 1162 and died in 1227.
　　　　4　Leonardo da Vinci was born in 1452 and died in 1519.
　　　　5　George Washington was born in 1732 and died in 1799.

28.3　1　died　　3　dead　　5　dead
　　　　2　death　　4　died

28.4　2　(bride)groom　　6　a funeral
　　　　3　single　　　　　7　a honeymoon
　　　　4　to weigh　　　　8　widowed
　　　　5　divorced

28.5　1　In　　3　of　　5　born
　　　　2　to　　4　on　　6　after

28.6 *Possible answer:*

I have two brothers and two sisters. My sisters are both married. One sister got married this year. She had a very big wedding and was a beautiful bride. They went to Italy on their honeymoon. The other sister got married four years ago. She has two children. The boy was born two years ago and the girl was born last year. One of my brothers is divorced and one is single. My father died two years ago. My mother is widowed.

Unit 29

29.1

2 brother.	6 grandfather.	10 wife.
3 aunt.	7 nephew.	11 cousin.
4 uncle.	8 niece.	
5 grandmother.	9 mother.	

29.2 *Possible family tree:*

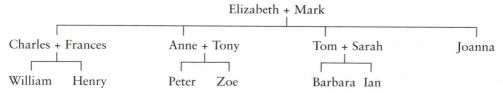

I am Tony. Anne is my wife. Peter and Zoe are our children. Peter is our son and Zoe is our daughter. Barbara is our niece. William, Henry and Ian are our nephews.

29.3

1 uncle	3 brother	5 grandsons	7 grandmother
2 aunt	4 father	6 cousins	8 daughter

29.4 *Possible answers:*

1 Chen has / has got one brother and one sister.
2 Chen has / has got two cousins.
3 Chen has / has got two nephews but I haven't got any nieces.
4 Chen has / has got only one grandmother now.

Unit 30

30.1

2 nose	4 stomach	6 ear
3 heart	5 shoulder	7 tooth

30.2 2 toes   3 teeth   4 nose   5 heart   6 ears   7 knee   8 blood

30.3
1 a back   b arms   c legs
2 The eye is the hole in the needle.
3 The face is the front of the clock (with the numbers on it). The big hand shows the minutes and the little hand shows the hours.
4 The neck is the narrow part at the top of the bottle.
5 The foot of the mountain is the bottom of the mountain (the lowest part).

30.4

2 football	5 headscarf
3 lipstick	6 handbag
4 hairbrush	

30.5 If you find you learnt the words with the pictures particularly well, then try, whenever possible, to draw a picture beside words you want to learn.

Unit 31

31.1 All the words fit into both columns except for *tie* – men; *skirt, dress, handbag* – women.

31.2
1 foot – shoe
2 finger – ring
3 legs – tights
4 eyes – glasses
5 waist – belt
6 head – hat
7 neck – scarf
8 hand – glove

31.3
1 is
2 is wearing
3 has; is carrying
4 is; are
5 were; are
6 Is

31.4
1 sunglasses
2 jersey
3 watch
4 skirt
5 brief-case
6 hat
7 shirt
8 coat
9 umbrella
10 boots

31.5 *Possible answer:*

I am wearing a blue T-shirt and black trousers. I have got white shoes on. I'm wearing a watch, three rings and a pair of glasses.

Unit 32

32.1
2 tall
3 slim/thin
4 fair
5 young
6 fat/overweight
7 elderly

32.2 *Possible questions:*

2 Is Elena's hair blonde/fair? Has Elena got blonde/fair hair? Does Elena have blonde/fair hair?
3 Is Mike's hair long? Does Mike have long hair? Has Mike got long hair?
4 Are your parents old? (*or* more polite: Are your parents elderly?)
5 Is his sister pretty/beautiful?
6 Why is Sara so thin? Why does Sara look so thin? Sara looks very thin, doesn't she?

32.3 *Possible answers:*

1 long blonde hair and fair skin.
2 short fair hair and a beard.
3 dark skin and dark hair.
4 long, has a moustache.

32.4 *Possible answers:*

Joanna: Joanna is tall. She has long black hair and brown eyes. She's very pretty.
Kevin: Kevin is medium height. He has fair hair and a beard. His eyes are blue. He's quite ordinary-looking.
My mother: My mother is short, with grey hair. She has green eyes. She is a beautiful woman.

Unit 33

33.1 *Possible answers:*

not serious	more serious	very serious
a headache a cold toothache	hay-fever asthma	cancer cholera a heart attack

33.2
1 I'm very well / I'm fine, thanks.
2 I feel sick. (*or perhaps* I don't feel very well. *or* I feel ill.)
3 feel ill.
4 I've got toothache.
5 a cold

33.3 *Possible answers:*
1 A lot of fruit and vegetables, not so many sweet things.
2 I like/love swimming/cycling/playing golf/skiing/jogging/playing tennis, etc.
3 Sometimes I have a lot of stress at work / when I have exams.
4 Yes, I had an operation once / I broke my leg, etc. ('Be in hospital' means you are ill, you are a patient. 'Be in **a** hospital' can just mean you are visiting someone.)

33.4
2 cholera
3 asthma
4 hay-fever
5 cancer / heart attacks (*or* heart disease)

Unit 34

34.1 *Possible answers:*
1 I love chocolate.
2 I hate cowboy films.
3 I like aeroplanes.
4 I like tea.
5 I don't like football.
6 I love cats.
7 I like cars.
8 I don't like jazz music.

34.2 *Possible answers:*
2 I prefer cats to dogs.
3 I prefer sightseeing to sunbathing.
4 I prefer BMWs to Rolls Royces.
5 I prefer strawberry to chocolate ice-cream.
6 I prefer watching sport to doing sport.

34.3 *Possible answers:*
2 I hope (that) the lesson ends soon.
3 I want some food.
4 I hope (that) my friend feels better soon.
5 I want to go to bed.
6 I want to cry.
7 I hope (that) it gets warmer soon.

34.4
2 is thirsty.
3 are happy.
4 is cold.
5 is tired.
6 is angry.
7 is surprised.

34.5 *Possible answers:*
2 I felt surprised yesterday when an old friend rang me.
3 I felt upset when my boss was rude to me.

Unit 35

35.1
1 Bless you!
2 Good luck!
3 Congratulations! / Well done!
4 Goodbye.
5 Happy Birthday!
6 Fine, thanks.
7 Hello! / Hi!
8 Thank you.

35.2
1 Excuse me!
2 Happy Christmas!
3 Sorry!
4 Congratulations!
5 Cheers!
6 Good morning!

35.3
1 Excuse me.
2 Thank you. Cheers!
3 Goodnight. Sleep well.
4 Good morning.
5 Good afternoon.
6 Happy New Year!
7 Sorry / Excuse me. I didn't understand.
8 Happy Christmas!

35.4

ANN:	Good evening.	ANN:	Would you like a drink?
BILL:	Good evening.	BILL:	Yes, please. A coke.
ANN:	How are you?	ANN:	With ice?
BILL:	Fine thanks. And you?*	BILL:	No, thanks.
ANN:	It's my birthday today.	ANN:	Here you are. Cheers.
BILL:	Happy Birthday.	BILL:	Cheers!

* You can say 'Terrible.' as Bill did, but usually we say 'Fine' even if we feel terrible.

35.5 *Possible answer:*

A: Hello, good morning.
B: Hi. How are you?
A: Fine thanks. And you?
B: Fine. A bit nervous. I'm taking my driving test today.
A: Good luck. That's funny, I passed mine last week.
B: Oh Congratulations!
A: It's my birthday today.
B: Is it? Happy Birthday. Why don't we go out for a drink this evening?
A: OK. See you later. Goodbye.
B: Goodbye. See you soon.

Unit 36

36.1
2 The Sahara is in Africa.
3 The Amazon is in South America.
4 Wogga Wogga is in Australia.
5 The Volga is in Europe.
6 Mount Kilimanjaro is in Africa.
7 The Mississippi is in North America.
8 Mount Fuji is in Asia.
9 Lake Titicaca is in South America.

36.2
1 China
2 Sweden
3 Thailand
4 Brazil
5 Spain
6 Russia

36.3 2 Rome is the capital of Italy.
3 Canberra is the capital of Australia.
4 Bogota is the capital of Colombia.
5 Cairo is the capital of Egypt.
6 Vienna is the capital of Austria.
7 Edinburgh is the capital of Scotland.
8 Ankara is the capital of Turkey.
9 Buenos Aires is the capital of Argentina.
10 Madrid is the capital of Spain.

36.4 Check your answers with your teacher if you are not sure.

36.5 2 In Mexico, Spain and Chile they speak Spanish but in Brazil they speak Portuguese.
3 In Austria, Germany and Switzerland they speak German but in Italy they speak Italian.
4 In Morocco, Egypt and Saudi Arabia they speak Arabic but in China they speak Chinese.
5 In Switzerland, Canada and France they speak French but in Scotland they speak English.

36.6
2 Vietnamese	6 German	10 Spanish	14 Greek
3 Korean	7 Egyptian	11 Peruvian	15 Australian
4 Thai	8 Argentinian	12 Chinese	16 Polish
5 Iraqi	9 Dutch	13 British	17 Indian

Unit 37

37.1 1 d 2 c 3 g 4 e 5 a 6 f 7 b

37.2 *Possible answer:*

most favourite = snow, sun, wind, rain, lightning, cloud, fog = least favourite

37.3 3 windy in La Paz.
4 is cloudy in Paris.
5 It is foggy in Tashkent.
6 It is sunny in Seoul. *or* The sun is shining in Seoul.
7 It is windy in Warsaw.
8 It is snowing in Washington.

37.4
1 shone	3 weather	5 lightning	7 storm
2 rains	4 snows	6 degrees	8 cold

37.5 *Possible answers:*

1 It sometimes snows in December.
2 It is usually 20 degrees in summer and 0 (zero) degrees in winter.
3 There are sometimes thunderstorms in August.
4 It is not usually very wet in spring.
5 We almost never have hurricanes.
6 Summer is my favourite season because it is warm and dry.

37.6 *Possible answer:*

Today it is sunny and warm. There are some clouds in the sky and a little wind. It is not raining and it is not snowing. There is no thunder or lightning – it is not hot enough.

Unit 38

38.1 2 At the tourist information office.   5 At the museum.
3 At the bank.   6 At the post office.
4 In/At the car park.

38.2 *Possible questions:*

2 Where's the town hall?
3 How do I get to the museum?
4 Is there a shopping centre?
5 Where can I park?
6 Where can I change money?

38.3 2 town hall   4 car park   6 pedestrian area
3 library   5 railway station   7 traffic warden

38.4 1 No parking (do not leave your car here)
2 No entry (you must not drive in)
3 Bus stop
4 Information

Unit 39

39.1 1 mountains   4 hills   7 wood   10 farm
2 forest   5 village   8 fields   11 country road
3 lake   6 path   9 river

39.2 1 on   2 cottage   3 village   4 town

39.3 1 We went swimming in the lake. The water was warm.
2 We went walking along a 5-kilometre path.
3 We went skiing down the mountain.
4 We saw some wonderful wildlife in the national park.
5 We had a picnic sitting by the river.

39.4 *Possible sentences:*

1 There are some big forests and a lot of farms.
2 There are no hills or mountains. The countryside is flat. There are a lot of paths where you
   can walk.
3 There is one big river and some small rivers. The wildlife there is very beautiful.
4 There are a lot of villages and some small towns.

39.5 1 /
2 the
3 the

Unit 40

40.1 *Possible answers:*

2 giraffe
3 Parrots; budgies; hens
4 Tigers; lions
5 horse; elephant
6 Fish; birds
7 meat
8 Hens; cows (*or* pigs)

40.2 sheep – lamb – lamb
cow – beef – calf
hen – chicken – chick
pig – pork – piglet

40.3 *Possible answers:*

1 Lions, tigers, monkeys, snakes, dogs and cats eat meat.
2 Cows, sheep, pigs, parrots (for feathers), snakes (for snakeskin). (You may think of some other things, e.g. horsehair for wigs for judges.)
3 Hen, tortoise, parrot, budgie, snake, fish.

40.4

Across	*Down*
3 cats	1 parrot
6 lion	2 monkey
7 horse	4 two sheep
8 elephant	5 tiger
	9 hen

40.5 Write down the number you remembered. Try again tomorrow and write down how many you remember then.

Unit 41

41.1 1 e   2 d   3 a   4 f   5 c   6 g   7 b

41.2 1 A single takes you to a place and a return takes you to that place and back again.
2 He or she checks what people bring into a country.
3 No, it lands at the end of a journey and takes off at the beginning of a journey.
4 You can get on a plane or a boat.
5 If you hire a car you have it for a day or a week. If you buy it it is your car.
6 No, you want to go somewhere in their car.

41.3 *Possible answer:*

At the airport, follow the signs to the railway station. Buy a ticket to Cambridge. There are trains every hour. At Cambridge station take a number 5 bus. The stop is just outside the station. Get off the bus at the hospital, cross the road and take the first road on the left. My house is on the corner of the street with a red door.

41.4 Keep the cards and test yourself every day. If you find this useful write cards for words from other units of the book.

41.5

Across	*Down*
3 map	1 timetable
6 helicopter	2 taxi
7 bus	3 motorcycle
8 petrol	4 platform
	5 train

Unit 42

42.1 1 b   2 c   3 a   4 d

42.2   *Possible answers:*

Entrance and Way In – cinema, museum, etc.
Exit and Way Out – airport, cinema, etc.
Push and Pull – on doors in public places e.g. shops, railway station, museum
Please ring for attention – at a hotel reception
Open and Closed – on the door of a shop or museum
Sale – on a shop window
Please pay here – in a shop
Queue this side – at a cinema
Please do not walk on the grass – in the garden of a palace, in some parks
Out of order – on a public phone, on a drinks machine, etc.
Toilets – in a restaurant
WC – in a hotel
Women and Men – in a café

42.3   2 No.   3 No.   4 a   5 b   6 Yes.

42.4   *Possible answers:*

Information	**Instructions**
Entrance and Way In	No smoking
Exit and Way Out	Please ring for attention
Push and Pull	Please pay here
Open and Closed	Queue this side
Sale	Please do not walk on the grass
Out of order	
Toilets	
WC	
Women and Men	

42.5   *Possible answers:*

You might see signs in English at airports, railways stations, beside the road, in hotels. Some other common signs are:
Stop
No entry
One way street
No parking
Admission free (= you don't need to pay to go in)

Unit 43

43.1   2 Fish … chips   5 meat
3 potatoes   6 a hot-dog
4 pasta/pizzas

43.2

fruit	*vegetables*
pineapple	beans
grapes	onions
apple	carrot
pear	garlic
	mushrooms

43.3　1 banana　　2 strawberry　　3 peas　　4 apple　　5 potatoes　　6 tomatoes

43.4　2 beer　　4 coffee　　6 mineral water
　　　　3 milk　　5 fruit juice

Unit 44

44.1　2 yes
　　　3 yes
　　　4 no, the freezer is *colder* than the fridge.
　　　5 yes
　　　6 no, a tea towel makes them *dry*.

44.2　*Possible questions:*
　　　1 Where's the coffee?
　　　　Where can I find the tea?
　　　2 Where's the saucepan?
　　　　Where's the frying pan?
　　　3 Where shall I put this mug?
　　　4 Can I help with the washing-up?

44.3　*Possible answers:*
　　　2 tea, a cup, a teapot, a spoon, maybe milk and sugar.
　　　3 an egg, a frying pan, oil, a cooker.
　　　4 a plate, a knife and fork, or a spoon and fork, or chopsticks.
　　　5 water and a glass or a cup or a mug.
　　　6 a microwave.

44.4　1 a microwave　　3 a frying pan and a glass
　　　2 a saucepan　　　4 a teapot

Unit 45

45.1　2 wardrobe　　　　5 alarm clock　　8 mirror
　　　3 chest of drawers　6 bedside lamp　9 comb
　　　4 bedside table　　7 brush

45.2　*Possible answers:*

　　　toothpaste, brush, comb, pyjamas, soap.

45.3　2 are washing their faces.
　　　3 is going downstairs.
　　　4 is having a bath.
　　　5 is getting dressed.
　　　6 is turning off the light.

45.4　*Possible answer:*

　　　bath, shower, toilet, basin, soap, shampoo, toothbrush, toothpaste, mirror, bathroom cupboard with medicines in it, shelf, plants.

45.5　*Possible answer:*

　　　In my bedroom there is a big bed. There are two wardrobes, one on the left and one on the right of the room. I have a bedside table with a lamp and an alarm clock on it. There is a cupboard beside the window. The cupboard has two shelves and five drawers in it.

Possible answer:

I usually go to bed at 10.30. I go upstairs to my bedroom. I get undressed and have a bath.
I am usually tired but I always read a bit. I turn off my light after ten minutes. I fall asleep
quickly. I wake up before my alarm clock rings. I get up when my alarm clock rings. I wash my
face, clean my teeth and get dressed. I go downstairs to the kitchen for breakfast.

Unit 46

46.1
2 a sofa
3 a coffee table, a side/small table
4 a picture

5 a light switch
6 a CD player/tape recorder
7 a carpet

46.2
1 a sofa/an armchair
2 switch on the reading lamp
3 use the remote control

46.3
1 On
2 in; on

3 near
4 against

5 in ... of

46.4 *Possible sentences:*

In my living room there is a table, a TV, a desk, a sofa and two armchairs. The TV is near the
window, and the sofa is against the wall. The table is in the middle of the room. The walls are
white and there are some pictures on them. I like to relax in the living room. In the evening I
watch TV there, or listen to music.

46.5

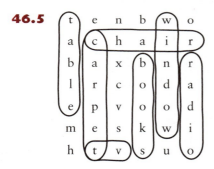

Unit 47

47.1
2 works in a hospital (or a clinic, or a surgery).
3 works in a restaurant (or a café).
4 works in an office.
5 works in a shop.
6 works in a hairdresser's (or a salon).

47.2   1 engineer   2 farmer   3 taxi-driver   4 nurse   5 mechanic   6 secretary

47.3 *Possible answers:*

1 I'm a teacher.
2 In a university.
3 Yes, very interesting.

47.4
Across
1 bus driver
2 teacher
3 writer

Down
1 doctor
2 waiter
3 nurse

Unit 48

48.1 1 c   2 d   3 g   4 f   5 b   6 i   7 e   8 a   9 h

48.2 *Possible answers:*

My three favourite subjects were languages, English and art. I didn't like physical education, physics and maths.

48.3 notebook, crayons, cassette, drawing pins, pencil, rubber, ruler, paper clip, tape recorder and pencil sharpener.

48.4 *Possible answer:*

I usually have a tape recorder and some cassettes, a notebook, some pens, some paper clips, a pencil, a rubber and a pencil sharpener.

48.5
2 did	6 taking	10 fails
3 passed	7 take/do	11 give
4 is studying	8 passes	
5 doing	9 get	

48.6 Try this exercise again in one week's time. How many words can you remember now?

Unit 49

49.1 *Possible answers:*

I have the following: address, letter, envelope, stamp, phone number, phone, mobile phone, computer, screen, disk, mouse, keyboard and e-mail address.

49.2
2 stamps	5 mouse	8 address
3 envelope	6 post box	9 screen
4 phone box	7 mobile phone	

49.3
1 It's	3 sorry	5 take/give him
2 speak	4 at	6 ring/call/phone

49.4 *Possible answers:*

1 01223 240754: oh one double two three, two four oh, seven five four
  0181 441 7895: oh one eight one, double four one, seven eight nine five
  01465 353607: oh one four six five, three five three, six oh seven
  01954 345882: oh one nine five four, three four five, double eight two
2 steve@stuff.co.uk: Steve at stuff dot co dot U-K
  TESL-L@cunyvm.cuny.edu: Tesl hyphen L at cuny V-M dot cuny dot edu (i.e. Tesl, cuny and edu are read as words while VM is read as individual letters)

49.5 *Possible answers:*

2 An e-mail is usually cheapest (if you have the equipment).
3 I've sent and received them all.
4 Phoning, because I like to talk to my friends.
5 E-mailing is quick and easy.

Unit 50

50.1 1 on   2 on   3 time   4 by

50.2
1 a package holiday (or package tour)	3 a walking holiday
2 a coach tour	4 a winter holiday / a skiing holiday

50.3 *Possible answers:*

	you can take a lot of luggage	*very fast*	*usually cheap*	*you see a lot as you travel*	*you can relax*
ferry	++		++	++	+++
car	+++	++	+++	+++	+
flight		+++	+	+	++

50.4 1 currency   2 passport   3 camera   4 luggage   5 phrase book   6 tickets

50.5 traveller's cheques; a visa

50.6 2 nightlife   3 local   4 Tourist Information   5 language

Unit 51

51.1 1 chemist's   3 butcher's   5 gift shop
2 toy shop   4 newsagent's   6 baker's

51.2 2 The hairdresser's.   5 A book shop.
3 The post office.   6 A department store (or a supermarket).
4 A gift shop.

51.3
1 3rd   5 1st   9 2nd
2 ground   6 basement   10 3rd
3 4th   7 ground   11 ground
4 basement   8 2nd   12 2nd

51.4
2 cash
3 a hairdresser
4 a credit card
5 the basement
6 a piece of paper that is worth five pounds
7 the floor above the ground floor (in a British building)
8 a piece of paper that you get when you buy something
9 the place where you pay for things in a shop

51.5 *Possible answers:*

Shops near me: baker's, newsagent's, chemist's, post office, hairdresser's, supermarket

Departments in my favourite department store: childrenswear, sports equipment, menswear, cosmetics, toys, ladieswear, shoes, electrical goods, stationery, furniture

51.6 1 cost   2 pay   3 (carrier) bag

Unit 52

52.1
1 double room   5 kettle
2 shower   6 sea
3 TV   7 key
4 telephone   8 lift

52.2 1 d   2 a   3 h   4 f   5 b   6 g   7 c   8 e

52.3 *Possible answers:*

1 From £30 – £80 per night
2 00 44 (from e.g. France)
3 8. 29
4 12
5 Because they are no use to a thief.

52.4 *Possible answer:*

YOU: Excuse me, please. Can I have one double and one single room for tonight?
RECEPTIONIST: With a bathroom?
YOU: Yes, please.
RECEPTIONIST: Rooms 11 and 12 are free. They are on the first floor.
YOU: How much are they?
RECEPTIONIST: The single room is £30 and the double is £50.
YOU: Thank you. That's fine. We'll take them.
RECEPTIONIST: Good. Can you fill in this form for me, please?

52.5 *Possible answer:*

Can I have a morning call, please?
Can I have breakfast in my room, please?
Can I book a room for next week, please?
Can I have a double room for tonight, please?
Can I have my bill, please?
Can I borrow a hairdryer, please?

Unit 53

53.1 *Possible answers:*

2 restaurant   4 café
3 fast food restaurant   5 bar/pub/café

53.2 *Possible answers:*

café – Jim's Corner Café
restaurant – The Taj Mahal
bar – The Red Lion
sandwich bar – Annabelle's
fast food restaurant – Burger King
self-service café – café in railway station

53.3 *Possible answers:*

1 I'd choose tomato soup, chicken salad and strawberries and cream.
2 A vegetarian would choose melon or tomato soup and a cheese or plain omelette and any of
   the desserts.

53.4 2 omelette   3 salad   4 potatoes   5 gateau   6 steak

53.5 WAITER: Are you ready to order?
        CUSTOMER: Yes. I'd like vegetable soup and steak, please.
        WAITER: How would you like your steak? Rare, medium or well-done?
        CUSTOMER: Rare, please.
        WAITER: What would you like to drink?
        CUSTOMER: An orange juice, please.

Unit 54

54.1
1 rugby	3 judo/karate	5 volleyball
2 cricket	4 sailing	6 motor racing

54.2
1 canoeing	3 badminton	5 table tennis
2 baseball	4 basketball	6 skiing

54.3
2 play football?
3 Do you do any sports?
4 go swimming? / like swimming? / swim?

Unit 55

55.1
2 Science fiction		6 Romance
3 Horror		7 Crime/Detective
4 Action		8 Musical
5 Cartoon		

55.2

```
            C R I M E
            H O R R O R
          C O M E D Y
              A C T I O N
    S C I E N C E F I C T I O N
          W E S T E R N
          M U S I C A L
              C A R T O O N
```

55.3
1 to the	3 played	5 film stars
2 watched (some people say 'saw a video')	4 in	6 director

55.4 *Possible answers:*

1 *Star Wars, Star Trek*, etc.
2 Sean Connery, Demi Moore, Arnold Schwarzenegger, etc.
3 Yes, I love them. No, they're boring.
  Dick Tracy is one example.
4 Yes, if I'm not on my own.

Unit 56

56.1
1 watching TV.	4 cooking.
2 gardening.	5 Internet.
3 reading, newspaper.	6 listening, CD.

56.2
2 read	5 have/invite	8 see/watch
3 talk	6 play	9 grows
4 have	7 watch	

56.3 *Possible answers:*

1 We talk, or we have a meal, or we listen to music, etc.
2 My best friend sometimes comes to stay. / My cousins sometimes come to stay, etc.
3 I like novels, and I read a newspaper every day.
4 I ring them about once a week.

56.4 *Possible answers for a young person who likes technology:*

◄──►

most interesting   *most boring*

using the Internet   watching videos   listening to music   doing nothing   reading   cooking   gardening

Unit 57

57.1 2 a murderer   4 a burglar   6 a drug pusher/dealer
         3 a shoplifter   5 a mugger

57.2 2 arrested   5 burglaries   8 terrorists
         3 vandals   6 innocent   9 prison
         4 fine   7 take

57.3 *Possible answers:*
         1 f   2 g   3 e   4 b   5 a   6 h   7 i

Unit 58

58.1 2 soap (opera) / talk show   4 nature   6 Internet
         3 documentary   5 teenage   7 comics

58.2 1 e   2 d   3 b   4 a   5 c

58.3 1 c   2 a   3 d   4 b

58.4 2 A journalist   4 A comic
         3 An evening (news)paper   5 A nature programme

58.5 *Possible answers:*
         1 I always read an evening newspaper.
         2 In Britain, most people have four or five channels. They have more if they have satellite TV.
         3 Satellite TV is getting more popular in Britain every year.
         4 I watch two or three hours every day.
         5 Documentaries and nature programmes.

Unit 59

59.1 2 Her computer has crashed.
         3 The cup is broken.
         4 The phone is out of order.
         5 She has too much work.
         6 His hand is cut.
         7 The room is untidy.
         8 She is late for work.

59.2 *Possible answers:*
         2 cut finger/hands/knees
         3 untidy room/desk/hair
         4 late for school / an appointment / a concert
         5 a camera/microwave/walkman that isn't working
         6 too much work/rain/wind

59.3 *Possible answers:*

Serious	*Not serious*
a computer crash	a TV that doesn't work
a broken washing machine	dying plants
lost keys	an untidy bedroom
a row with a friend	a cut finger
being late for work	a colleague in a bad mood
too much work	a photocopier that is out-of-order
a coffee machine that isn't working!	

59.4 *Possible answers:*

too much work – get an assistant
a colleague in a bad mood – pay no attention
a crashed computer – get a technician
a photocopier that is out-of-order – repair the photocopier
a coffee machine that isn't working – drink water

59.5 *Possible answers:*

My video recorder doesn't work.
My brother lost his credit card.
My husband broke a glass.

Unit 60

60.1

2 car crash	5 earthquake	8 traffic jam
3 flood	6 forest fire	9 snowstorm
4 war	7 hurricane	

60.2 *Possible answers:*

snowstorm – Alaska	earthquake – Japan
forest fire – Australia	flood – Bangladesh

60.3 *Possible answers:*

We have poor people in big cities, hungry people in big cities, homeless people in the capital, unemployed people in the north, too many people in the capital, traffic jams in big cities, car crashes on main roads, strikes in some factories. Fortunately, we don't have any wars.

60.4 *Possible answers:*

hurricane, snowstorm, flood – problems because of the weather
earthquake, car crash – things get smashed
forest fire, pollution, traffic jam – they make the environment dirty
poor, unemployed, hungry and homeless people – too many people
strike, war – problems caused by government and politics

60.5

2 strike	4 car crash	6 homeless
3 War	5 earthquakes; snowstorms	

Phonetic symbols

Vowel sounds

Symbol	Examples
/iː/	sleep me
/i/	happy recipe
/ɪ/	pin dinner
/ʊ/	foot could pull
/uː/	do shoe through
/e/	red head said
/ə/	arrive father colour
/ɜː/	turn bird work
/ɔː/	sort thought walk
/æ/	cat black
/ʌ/	sun enough wonder
/ɒ/	got watch sock
/ɑː/	part heart laugh
/eɪ/	name late aim
/aɪ/	my idea time
/ɔɪ/	boy noise
/eə/	pair where bear
/ɪə/	hear beer
/əʊ/	go home show
/aʊ/	out cow
/ʊə/	pure fewer

Consonant sounds

Symbol	Examples
/p/	put
/b/	book
/t/	take
/d/	dog
/k/	car kick
/g/	go guarantee
/tʃ/	catch church
/dʒ/	age lounge
/f/	for cough photograph
/v/	love vehicle
/θ/	thick path
/ð/	this mother
/s/	since rice
/z/	zoo houses
/ʃ/	shop sugar machine
/ʒ/	pleasure usual vision
/h/	hear hotel
/m/	make
/n/	name now know
/ŋ/	bring
/l/	look while
/r/	road
/j/	young
/w/	wear

Index

body /'bɒdi/ 30

book /bʊk/ 9, 38, 41, 52, 56

bookshelf /'bʊkʃelf/ 46

book shop /'bʊk ʃɒp/ 51

boot /buːt/ 2

boots /buːts/ 31

boring /'bɔːrɪŋ/ 55

born /bɔːn/ 28

borrow /'bɒrəʊ/ 27

bottom /'bɒtəm/ 18

bowl /bəʊl/ 44

brain /breɪn/ 30

Brazil /brə'zɪl/ 36

bread /bred/ 21, 43, 51

break /breɪk/ 20

break into /breɪk 'ɪntə/ 57

breakfast /'brekfəst/ 3, 6, 12, 45, 52

bride /braɪd/ 28

bridegroom /'braɪdgrʊm/ 28

briefcase /'briːfkeɪs/ 31

bring /brɪŋ/ 9, 20

British /'brɪtɪʃ/ 36

broken /'brəʊkən/ 59

brother /'brʌðə/ 29

brown /braʊn/ 32

budgie /'bʌdʒi/ 40

buffet /'bʊfeɪ/ 41

burger /'bɜːgə/ 53

burglar /'bɜːglə/ 57

burglary /'bɜːgləri/ 57

bus /bʌs/ 8, 10, 14, 38, 41, 50

bust /bʌst/ 30

but /bʌt/ 15

butcher('s) /'bʊtʃə(z)/ 51

butter /'bʌtə/ 21

buy /baɪ/ 20

by /baɪ/ 2

café /'kæfeɪ/ 53

cakes /keɪks/ 51

calf /kɑːf/ 40

call /kɔːl/ 12, 28, 49

camera /'kæmrə/ 8, 50

Canada /'kænədə/ 36

Canadian /kə'neɪdiən/ 36

cancer /'kænsə/ 36

canoeing /kə'nuːɪŋ/ 54

car /kɑː/ 2, 14, 38, 41, 50

car crash /'kɑː kræʃ/ 60

car park /'kɑː pɑːk/ 38

car theft /'kɑː θeft/ 57

car thief /'kɑː θiːf/ 57

carpet /'kɑːpɪt/ 46

carrier bag /'kæriə bæg/ 51

carrot(s) /'kærət(s)/ 43, 53

carry /'kæri/ 14, 31

cartoon /kɑː'tuːn/ 55, 58

cash /kæʃ/ 51, 52

cash desk /'kæʃ desk/ 51

cassette /kə'set/ 48

cat /kæt/ 40

catch /kætʃ/ 14, 20

CD /siː'diː/ 46, 56

centre /'sentə/ 38

century /'sentʃəri/ 16

chair /tʃeə/ 2, 46

chance /tʃɑːns/ 8

change /tʃeɪndʒ/ 41, 51, 52

channel /'tʃænəl/ 58

check /tʃek/ 27, 41, 52

check in /tʃek 'ɪn/ 41

check out /tʃek 'aʊt/ 52

Cheers /tʃɪəz/ 35

cheese /tʃiːz/ 53

chemist('s) /'kemɪst(s)/ 51

chemistry /'kemɪstri/ 48

cheque /tʃek/ 51

chest /tʃest/ 30

chick /tʃɪk/ 40

chicken /'tʃɪkɪn/ 40, 53

childrenswear /'tʃɪldrənzweə/ 51

China /'tʃaɪnə/ 36

Chinese /tʃaɪ'niːz/ 36

chips /tʃɪps/ 53

chocolate /'tʃɒklət/ 53

cholera /'kɒlərə/ 33

choose /tʃuːz/ 20

chopsticks /'tʃɒpstɪks/ 44

church /tʃɜːtʃ/ 28

cinema /'sɪnəmə/ 55

clean /kliːn/ 12

clean your teeth /kliːn jə 'tiːθ/ 45

climb /klaɪm/ 14

close /kləʊz/ 46

closed /kləʊzd/ 42

clothes /kləʊðz/ 2, 12, 31, 51

cloud /klaʊd/ 37

cloudy /'klaʊdi/ 37

coach tour /'kəʊtʃ tʊə/ 50

coat /kəʊt/ 31

code /kəʊd/ 52

coffee /'kɒfi/ 3, 6, 10, 21, 43

coffee maker /'kɒfi meɪkə/ 44

coffee machine /'kɒfi mə'ʃiːn/ 59

coffee table /'kɒfi teɪbəl/ 46

cold /kəʊld/ 2, 33, 34, 37

college /'kɒlɪdʒ/ 47

collocation /kɒlə'keɪʃn/ 2

colour /'kʌlə/ 51

column /'kɒləm/ 1

comb /kəʊm/ 45

come /kʌm/ 7, 12, 20, 56

come back / in / out of /kʌm bæk / ɪn / aʊt əv/ 7

come on /kʌm ɒn/ 11

comedy /'kɒmədi/ 55

comic /'kɒmɪk/ 58

communication /kəmjuːnɪ'keɪʃn/ 49

competition /kɒmpə'tɪʃn/ 3

complete /kəm'pliːt/ 1

computer /kəm'pjuːtə/ 48, 49, 58

computer game /kəmp'juːtə geɪm/ 56

congratulations /kəngrætʃuː'leɪʃnz/ 13, 55

conjunction /kən'dʒʌŋkʃn/ 15

conservation area /kɒnsə'veɪʃn 'eəriə/ 39

continent /'kɒntɪnənt/ 36

control /kən'trəʊl/ 27

cook /kʊk/ 27

cooker /'kʊkə/ 26, 27, 44

cooking /'kʊkɪŋ/ 56

cool /kuːl/ 2

copy /'kɒpi/ 6
corner /'kɔːnə/ 46
correct /kə'rekt/ 1
cosmetics /kɒz'metɪks/ 51
cost /kɒst/ 20, 51, 52
cottage /'kɒtɪdʒ/ 39
countable /'kaʊntəbəl/ 21
country /'kʌntri/ 36, 39
countryside /'kʌntrɪsaɪd/
    39
course /kɔːs/ 8, 48, 53
court /kɔːt/ 54, 57
cousin /'kʌzən/ 29
cow /kaʊ/ 40
crash /kræʃ/ 59
crayon /'kreɪɒn/ 48
cream /kriːm/ 53
credit card /'kredɪt kaːd/
    51
cricket /'krɪkɪt/ 54
crime /kraɪm/ 55, 57
crowded /'kraʊdɪd/ 60
cry /kraɪ/ 2
cup /kʌp/ 2, 3
cupboard /'kʌbəd/ 44, 45
currency /'kʌrənsi/ 50, 52
curtain /'kɜːtən/ 46
customs /'kʌstəmz/ 41
cut /kʌt/ 20, 59

dance /daːns/ 14
dark /daːk/ 2, 10, 32
date /deɪt/ 49
daughter /'dɔːtə/ 29
day /deɪ/ 12, 16
day after tomorrow /deɪ
    aːftə tə'mɒrəʊ/ 16
day before yesterday /deɪ
    bɪfɔː 'jestədeɪ/ 16
dead /ded/ 28
death /deθ/ 28
December /dɪ'sembə/ 16
degree /dɪ'griː/ 48
degrees /dɪ'griːz/ 37
dentist /'dentɪst/ 3, 33
depart /dɪ'paːt/ 41
department store
    /dɪ'paːtmənt stɔː/ 51
desk /desk/ 2, 48
dessert /dɪ'zɜːt/ 53
detective /dɪ'tektɪv/ 55

dialogue /'daɪəlɒg/ 1
die /daɪ/ 28, 59
diet /'daɪət/ 33
different /'dɪfrənt/ 51
difficult /'dɪfɪkəlt/ 23
dinner /'dɪnə/ 3, 6, 12, 52,
    56
director /daɪ'rektə/ 55
disaster /dɪ'zaːstə/ 60
disk /dɪsk/ 49
dishes /'dɪʃɪz/ 6
dislike /dɪs'laɪk/ 34
divorced /dɪ'vɔːst/ 28
do /duː/ 2, 5, 20, 54, 56
do a course /duː ə kɔːs/
    48
do business with /duː
    'bɪznɪs wɪð/ 5
do homework /duː
    'həʊmwɜːk/ 5, 48
do some exercises /duː səm
    'eksəsaɪsɪz/ 5
do the gardening /duː ðə
    'gaːdnɪŋ/ 5
do the housework /duː ðə
    haʊswɜːk/ 5
do the washing /duː ðə
    wɒʃɪŋ/ 5
do the washing-up /duː ðə
    wɒʃɪŋ 'ʌp/ 5
do up /duː 'ʌp/ 11
do your best /duː jə 'best/
    5
doctor /'dɒktə/ 5, 6, 10,
    33, 47
documentary
    /dɒkjə'mentri/ 58
dog /dɒg/ 40
doll /dɒl/ 51
door /dɔː/ 2, 13
double room /dʌbəl 'ruːm/
    52
downstairs /daʊn'steəz/
    45
draw /drɔː/ 46
drawers /drɔːz/ 45
drawing pin /'drɔːɪŋ pɪn/
    48
dress /dres/ 2, 31
dressing table /'dresɪŋ
    teɪbəl/ 45

drink /drɪŋk/ 2, 20, 43, 53
drive /draɪv/ 14, 20
drug pusher /'drʌg pʊʃə/
    57
drug pushing /'drʌg pʊʃɪŋ/
    57
dry /draɪ/ 2, 37
Dutch /dʌtʃ/ 36

ear /ɪə/ 30
earthquake /'ɜːθkweɪk/ 60
easy-going /iːzi 'gəʊɪŋ/ 23
eat /iːt/ 2, 20, 53
economics /iːkə'nɒmɪks/
    26
egg /eg/ 40
Egypt /'iːdʒɪpt/ 36
Egyptian /ɪ'dʒɪpʃn/ 36
elderly /'eldəli/ 32
electrical goods /ɪ'lektrɪkəl
    gʊdz/ 51
elephant /'elɪfənt/ 40
e-mail /'iː meɪl/ 49
end /end/ 8, 18
endless /'endləs/ 26
engineer /endʒɪ'nɪə/ 5, 47
English /'ɪŋglɪʃ/ 36, 48,
    54
enjoy /ɪn'dʒɔɪ/ 55
entrance /'entrəns/ 42
envelope /'envələʊp/ 49
Europe /'jʊərəp/ 36
even /'iːvən/ 15
evening /'iːvnɪŋ/ 16, 27
every /'evri/ 12
everyday /'evrideɪ/ 59
everywhere /'evriweə/ 18
exam /ɪg'zæm/ 2, 3, 6, 8,
    48
example /ɪg'zaːmpəl/ 1
excellent /'eksələnt/ 22
exchange /ɪks'tʃeɪndʒ/ 52
excuse me /ɪk'skjuːz miː/
    35, 38
exercise /'eksəsaɪz/ 2, 33
ex-husband /eks 'hʌzbənd/
    25
exit /'eksɪt/ 42
expect /ɪk'spekt/ 27
ex-president /eks
    'prezɪdənt/ 25

ex-wife /eks 'waɪf/ 25
eye /aɪ/ 30

face /feɪs/ 30, 32
factory /'fæktri/ 47
fail /feɪl/ 48
fair /feə/ 32
fall /fɔːl/ 14, 20, 27
fall asleep /fɔːl ə'sliːp/ 45
family /'fæməli/ 29
fare /feə/ 41
farm /fɑːm/ 39
farmer /'fɑːmə/ 39, 47
fast /fɑːst/ 19, 26
fast food /fɑːst 'fuːd/ 43
fast food restaurant /'fɑːst
  fuːd 'restrɒnt/ 53
fat /fæt/ 32
father /'fɑːðə/ 29
favourite /'feɪvərɪt/ 54
fax /fæks/ 49
February /'februəri/ 16
feel /fiːl/ 6, 20, 27
feelings /'fiːlɪŋz/ 34
feet /fiːt/ 30
ferry /'feri/ 50
field /'fiːld/ 39
fight /faɪt/ 20
fill /fɪl/ 1
fill in a form /fɪl ɪn ə
  'fɔːm/ 52
fill up with /fɪl 'ʌp wɪð/
  41
film /fɪlm/ 6, 55, 58
film star /'fɪlm stɑː/ 55
find /faɪnd/ 20
fine /faɪn/ 33, 35, 57
finger /'fɪŋgə/ 30
Finnish /'fɪnɪʃ/ 36
first floor /fɜːst 'flɔː/ 51,
  52
fish /fɪʃ/ 40, 43, 53
fish and chips /fɪʃ ən
  'tʃɪps/ 43
flight /flaɪt/ 41
flood /flʌd/ 60
floor /flɔː/ 51
flower /'flaʊə/ 9, 56
fly /flaɪ/ 14, 20, 50
fog /fɒg/ 37
foggy /'fɒgi/ 37

food /fuːd/ 21, 43, 50, 51
foot /fʊt/ 30
football /'fʊtbɔːl/ 3, 30,
  54
footballer /'fʊtbɔːlə/ 26
football hooligan /'fʊtbɔːl
  'huːlɪgən/ 57
football hooliganism
  /'fʊtbɔːl 'huːlɪgənɪzm/
  57
forest /'fɒrɪst/ 39
forest fire /fɒrɪst 'faɪə/ 60
forget /fə'get/ 20, 49
fork /fɔːk/ 2, 44
form /fɔːm/ 9, 52
formal /'fɔːməl/ 25
fortnight /'fɔːtnaɪt/ 16
fourth floor /fɔːθ 'flɔː/ 51
France /frɑːns/ 36
freezer /'friːzə/ 44
French /frentʃ/ 36
Friday /'fraɪdeɪ/ 16
fridge /frɪdʒ/ 44
friend /frend/ 12, 56
friendly /'frendli/ 19
front /frʌnt/ 18
fruit /fruːt/ 43
fruit juice /'fruːt dʒuːs/ 43
fruit salad /fruːt 'sæləd/
  53
frying pan /'fraɪɪŋ pæn/ 44
funeral /'fjuːnərəl/ 28
furniture /'fɜːnɪtʃə/ 2, 21,
  51
future /'fjuːtʃə/ 17

game /geɪm/ 3, 51
gap /gæp/ 1
garden /'gɑːdən/ 9, 56
gardening /'gɑːdənɪŋ/ 56
garlic /'gɑːlɪk/ 43
gateau /'gætəʊ/ 53
geography /dʒi'ɒgrəfi/ 48
German /'dʒɜːmən/ 36
Germany /'dʒɜːməni/ 36
get /get/ 10, 20
get a degree /get ə dɪ'griː/
  48
get accustomed / used to
  /get ə'kʌstəmd /
  'juːs tə/ 48

get back /get 'bæk/ 10
get dressed /get 'drest/
  31, 45
get married /get 'mærɪd/
  10, 28
get on /get 'ɒn/ 11
get over /get 'əʊvə/ 11
get to /'get tə/ 14
get undressed /get
  ʌn'drest/ 31, 45
get up /get 'ʌp/ 10, 11, 12,
  45
gift shop /'gɪft ʃɒp/ 51
giraffe /dʒɪ'rɑːf/ 40
give /gɪv/ 20
give a lecture /gɪv ə
  'lektʃə/ 48
glass /glɑːs/ 29, 44
glasses /'glɑːsɪz/ 31
global /'gləʊbəl/ 60
gloves /glʌvz/ 31
go /gəʊ/ 4, 12, 20, 54,
  55
go away /gəʊ ə'weɪ/ 4
go back /gəʊ 'bæk/ 4
go by /gəʊ 'baɪ/ 14
go camping /gəʊ 'kæmpɪŋ/
  50
go dancing / fishing /
  sightseeing / swimming
  etc. /gəʊ 'dɑːnsɪŋ/
  'fɪʃɪŋ/ 'saɪtsiːɪŋ /
  'swɪmɪŋ/ 4
go down /gəʊ 'daʊn/ 4
go for a walk /gəʊ fə ə
  'wɔːk/ 12
go in /gəʊ 'ɪn/ 4
go into /gəʊ 'ɪntə/ 4
go off /gəʊ 'ɒf/ 11
go on /gəʊ 'ɒn/ 11
go out of /gəʊ 'aʊt əv/ 4
go shopping /gəʊ 'ʃɒpɪŋ/
  4, 51
go skiing / walking /gəʊ
  'skiːɪŋ / 'wɔːkɪŋ/ 4, 39
go through /gəʊ 'θruː/ 41
go to bed /gəʊ tə 'bed/ 12,
  45
go up /gəʊ 'ʌp/ 4
going to /'gəʊɪŋ tə/ 4
good /gʊd/ 19, 22, 23

good morning / afternoon / evening / night /gʊd 'mɔːnɪŋ / ɑːftə'nuːn/ 'iːvnɪŋ / naɪt/ 35

good at /gʊd ət/ 2, 24

good luck /gʊd 'lʌk/ 35

goodbye /gʊd'baɪ/ 13, 35

grammar /'græmə/ 1

granddaughter /'grændɔːtə/ 29

grandfather /'grænfɑːðə/ 28, 29

grandmother /'grænmʌðə/ 29

grandparents /'grænpeərənts/ 29

grandson /'grænsʌn/ 29

grape /greɪp/ 43

great /greɪt/ 22

Greece /griːs/ 36

Greek /griːk/ 36

green peas /griːn 'piːz/ 53

green /griːn/ 32

greetings /'griːtɪŋz/ 35

groom /gruːm/ 28

ground floor /graʊnd 'flɔː/ 51

grow /grəʊ/ 56

guilty /'gɪlti/ 57

guitar /gɪ'tɑː/ 9

hair dresser('s) /heə 'dresə(z)/ 47, 51

hair dryer /'heə draɪə/ 52

hair /heə/ 30, 32

hairbrush /'heəbrʌʃ/ 30, 45

half-brother /hɑːf 'brʌðə/ 25

half-hour /hɑːf 'aʊə/ 25

half-price /hɑːf 'praɪs/ 25

ham /hæm/ 40, 53

hamburger /'hæmbɜːgə/ 43

hand /hænd/ 18, 30

handbag /'hænbæg/ 30, 31

handsome /'hænsəm/ 32

happily /'hæpɪli/ 26

happiness /'hæpɪnəs/ 26

happy /'hæpi/ 2, 23, 34

Happy Birthday /hæpi 'bɜːθdeɪ/ 13, 35

Happy Christmas /hæpi 'krɪsməs/ 35

Happy New Year /'hæpi njuː jɪə/ 13, 35

hardly ever /hɑːdli: 'evə/ 17

hat /hæt/ 2, 31

hate /heɪt/ 34

have /hæv/ 3, 12, 20, 56

have (your) hair cut /hæv (jə) 'heə kʌt/ 3

have a baby /hæv ə 'beɪbi/ 28

have a go /hæv ə 'gəʊ/ 3

have a good time /'hæv ə gʊd 'taɪm/ 3

have a look /hæv ə 'lʊk/ 3

have a moment /hæv ə 'məʊmənt/ 3

have a row with /hæv ə 'raʊ wɪð/ 59

have a shower /hæv ə 'ʃaʊə/ 45

have a word with /hæv ə 'wɜːd wɪð/ 3

have got /həv gɒt/ 3

have got... on /həv gɒt... ɒn/ 31

have the time /hæv ðə 'taɪm/ 3

have to /'hæv tə/ 3

hayfever /'heɪ fiːvə/ 33

head /hed/ 30, 32

headache /'hedeɪk/ 33

headlight /'hedlaɪt/ 2

headscarf /'hedskɑːf/ 30

health /helθ/ 33

hear /hɪə/ 20

heart /hɑːt/ 30

heart attack /'hɑːt ətæk/ 28, 33

height /haɪt/ 32

helicopter /'helɪkɒptə/ 41

hello /hel'əʊ/ 13, 35

hen /hen/ 40

here /hɪə/ 7, 9, 18

hi /haɪ/ 35

high /haɪ/ 2

hill /hɪl/ 39

hips /hɪps/ 30

hire /haɪə/ 41

history /'hɪstri/ 48

hobby /'hɒbi/ 56

holiday /'hɒlədeɪ/ 50

Holland /'hɒlənd/ 36

home /həʊm/ 7, 10, 12, 18, 47, 56

homeless /'həʊmləs/ 60

homework /'həʊmwɜːk/ 3, 6, 48

honeymoon /'hʌnimuːn/ 28

hooligan /'huːlɪgən/ 57

hope /həʊp/ 27

hopeful /'həʊpfəl/ 26

horrible /'hɒrəbəl/ 22, 23

horror /'hɒrə/ 55

horse /hɔːs/ 14, 40

horse racing /'hɔːs reɪsɪŋ/ 54

hospital /'hɒspɪtəl/ 33, 47

hot /hɒt/ 2, 34, 37

hot chocolate /hɒt 'tʃɒklət/ 6

hot-dog /'hɒt dɒg/ 43

hotel /həʊ'tel/ 52

hour /aʊə/ 16

house /haʊs/ 9, 12

house plant /'haʊs plɑːnt/ 56

how...! /haʊ/ 22

how are you? /haʊ ɑː 'juː/ 35

how do I get to...? /haʊ də waɪ 'get tə/ 38

how do you...? /'haʊ djə/ 12

how often...? /haʊ 'ɒfən/ 12

hungry /'hʌngri/ 34, 60

hurricane /'hʌrɪkən/ 37, 60

hurt /hɜːt/ 20

husband /'hʌzbənd/ 29

ice /aɪs/ 2

ice-cream /aɪs 'kriːm/ 53

Icelandic /aɪs'lændɪk/ 36

if /ɪf/ 15

ill /ɪl/ 10, 28, 33, 34

illness /'ɪlnəs/ 33

impossible /ɪm'pɒsəbəl/ 25

in /ɪn/ 55

in a bad mood /ɪn ə bæd 'muːd/ 59

in a moment /ɪn ə 'məʊmənt/ 17

in advance /ɪn əd'vaːns/ 41

incorrect /ɪnkə'rekt/ 25

India /'ɪndɪə/ 36

informal /ɪn'fɔːməl/ 25

information /ɪnfə'meɪʃn/ 21

information technology /ɪnfə'meɪʃn tek'nɒlədʒi/ 48

innocent /'ɪnəsənt/ 57

instructions /ɪn'strʌkʃnz/ 1

instructor /ɪn'strʌktə/ 26

intelligent /ɪn'telɪdʒənt/ 23

interested in /'ɪntrestɪd ɪn/ 24

Internet /'ɪntənet/ 56, 58

interview /'ɪntəvjuː/ 58

invite /ɪn'vaɪt/ 56

Iraqi /ɪ'raːki/ 36

Irish /'aɪrɪʃ/ 36

irregular verb /ɪ'regjələ 'vɜːb/ 20

Israeli /ɪz'reɪli/ 36

Italy /'ɪtəli/ 36

jacket /'dʒækɪt/ 31

Jamaican /dʒə'meɪkən/ 36

January /'dʒænjʊəri/ 16

Japan /dʒə'pæn/ 36

Japanese /dʒæpə'niːz/ 8, 13, 36

jeans /dʒiːnz/ 31

job /dʒɒb/ 10, 47

jog /dʒɒg/ 14

joke /dʒəʊk/ 13

journalist /'dʒɜːnəlɪst/ 58

journey /'dʒɜːni/ 3, 41

judo /'dʒuːdəʊ/ 54

juice /dʒuːs/ 53

July /dʒə'laɪ/ 16

jump /dʒʌmp/ 14

jumper /'dʒʌmpə/ 31

June /dʒuːn/ 16

karate /kə'raːti/ 54

keep /kiːp/ 20

kettle /'ketəl/ 52

key /kiː/ 52

keyboard /'kiːbɔːd/ 49

kind /kaɪnd/ 23

kitchen /'kɪtʃɪn/ 44

kitchen paper /'kɪtʃɪn 'peɪpə/ 44

knee /niː/ 30

knife /naɪf/ 2, 44

know /nəʊ/ 20

Korea /kə'riːə/ 36

Korean /kə'rɪən/ 36

ladieswear /'leɪdɪzweə/ 51

lake /leɪk/ 39

lamb /læm/ 40

land /lænd/ 2, 41

language /'læŋgwɪdʒ/ 1, 36, 50

languages /'læŋgwɪdʒɪz/ 48

last /laːst/ 17

late for /'leɪt fə/ 59

learn /lɜːn/ 20, 48

leather /'leðə/ 40

leave /liːv/ 20

lecture /'lektʃə/ 48

left /left/ 1, 18

leg /leg/ 30

leisure /'leʒə/ 56

lend /lend/ 27

lesson /'lesən/ 3, 8

let /let/ 20

letter /'letə/ 49

letters /'letəz/ 12

library /'laɪbrəri/ 38

lift /lɪft/ 52

light /laɪt/ 10, 45

lightning /'laɪtnɪŋ/ 37

like /laɪk/ 15, 34, 54

lion /'laɪən/ 40

lip /lɪp/ 30

lipstick /'lɪpstɪk/ 30

listen (to) /'lɪsən (tə)/ 12, 24, 46, 56

living room /'lɪvɪŋ rʊm/ 46

local /'ləʊkəl/ 50

look /lʊk/ 8

look after /lʊk 'aːftə/ 24

look at /'lʊk ət/ 24

look for /'lʊk fə/ 24, 38, 59

look forward to /lʊk 'fɔːwəd tə/ 24

loose /luːs/ 27

lose /luːz/ 20, 27, 59

loud /laʊd/ 19

love /lʌv/ 34, 55

love story /'lʌv stɔːri/ 55

lovely /'lʌvli/ 22, 23

luggage /'lʌgɪdʒ/ 21, 41, 50, 52

lunch /lʌntʃ/ 3, 6, 52

magazine /mægə'ziːn/ 56, 58

magazines /mægə'ziːnz/ 51

main course /'meɪn kɔːs/ 53

make /meɪk/ 2, 6, 12, 20

make a (phone) call /meɪk ə 'fəʊn kɔːl/ 49

malaria /mə'leərɪə/ 33

man-made /'mæn meɪd/ 60

manner /'mænə/ 19

map /mæp/ 41

March /maːtʃ/ 16

marriage /'mærɪdʒ/ 28

married /'mærɪd/ 28

mashed potatoes /mæʃt pə'teɪtəʊz/ 53

match /mætʃ/ 1

mathematics (maths) /mæθ'mætɪks/ 26, 48

May /meɪ/ 16

meal /miːl/ 3, 53

meat /miːt/ 40, 43, 51

mechanic /mɪ'kænɪk/ 5, 47

media /'miːdɪə/ 58

medicine /'medsən/ 51

medium /'miːdɪəm/ 32, 53

meet /miːt/ 20

meeting /'miːtɪŋ/ 3

melon /'melən/ 53

men /men/ 42

mend /mend/ 59

menswear /'menzweə/ 51

menu /'menjuː/ 53

Merry Christmas /meri
'krɪsməs/ 13, 35

message /'mesɪdʒ/ 49

metro /'metrəʊ/ 8

Mexican /'meksɪkən/ 36

Mexico /'meksɪkəʊ/ 36

microwave /'maɪkrəʊweɪv/
44

middle /'mɪdəl/ 18, 46

middle-aged /mɪdəl 'eɪdʒd/
32

milk /mɪlk/ 21, 40, 43

mineral water /'mɪnərəl
'wɔːtə/ 43

minus /'maɪnəs/ 37

minute /'mɪnɪt/ 8, 16

mirror /'mɪrə/ 45

miss /mɪs/ 14

mistake /mɪs'teɪk/ 6

mixed /mɪkst/ 53

mobile phone
/məʊbaɪl 'fəʊn/ 49

moment /'məʊmənt/ 17

Monday /'mʌndeɪ/ 16

money /'mʌni/ 21, 38, 52

monkey /'mʌŋki/ 40

month /mʌnθ/ 16

mood /muːd/ 59

morning /'mɔːnɪŋ/ 16, 58

morning call /mɔːnɪŋ 'kɔːl/
52

mother /'mʌðə/ 29

motor racing /'məʊtə
reɪsɪŋ/ 54

motorbike /'məʊtəbaɪk/
14, 41

motorcycle /'məʊtəsaɪkəl/
41

motorway /'məʊtəweɪ/
18

mountain /'maʊntɪn/ 39

mouse /maʊs/ 49

moustache /mə'staːʃ/ 32

mouth /maʊθ/ 30

move /muːv/ 14

mug /mʌg/ 2, 44, 57

mugger /'mʌgə/ 57

mugging /'mʌgɪŋ/ 57

murder /'mɜːdə/ 57

murderer /'mɜːdərə/ 57

museum /mjuː'ziːəm/ 8,
38

music centre /'mjuːzɪk
'sentə/ 46

music /'mjuːzɪk/ 48, 56

musical /'mjuːzɪkəl/ 55

nail /neɪl/ 30

name /neɪm/ 13

national park /'næʃənəl
'paːk/ 39

natural disaster /'nætʃərəl
dɪ'zaːstə/ 60

nature /'neɪtʃə/ 39, 58

naughty /'nɔːti/ 23

near /nɪə/ 46

neck /nek/ 30

negative /'negətɪv/ 23

Nepalese /nepə'liːz/ 36

nephew /'nefjuː/ 29

never /'nevə/ 17

New Zealand /njuː
'ziːlənd/ 36

news /njuːz/ 21, 58

newsagent('s)
/'njuːzeɪdʒənt(s)/ 51

newspaper /'njuːspeɪpə/
10, 38, 51, 56

next /nekst/ 17

next to /'neks tə/ 46

nice /naɪs/ 22, 23

niece /niːs/ 29

night /naɪt/ 27

night life /'naɪt laɪf/ 50

nightdress /'naɪtdres/ 45

nightie /'naɪti/ 45

no entry /nəʊ 'entri/ 38

no parking /nəʊ 'paːkɪŋ/
38

no smoking /nəʊ
'sməʊkɪŋ/ 42

noise /nɔɪz/ 6

non-smoking /nɒn
'sməʊkɪŋ/ 25

normally /'nɔːməli/ 12

North America /nɔːθ
ə'merɪkə/ 36

Norway /'nɔːweɪ/ 36

Norwegian /nɔː'wiːdʒən/
36

nose /nəʊz/ 30

not too bad /nɒt tuː 'bæd/
35

note /nəʊt/ 51

notebook /'nəʊtbʊk/ 48

nothing /'nʌθɪŋ/ 56

notice /'nəʊtɪs/ 42

noticeboard /'nəʊtɪsbɔːd/
48

noun /naʊn/ 1

novel /'nɒvəl/ 56

November /nəʊ'vembə/
16

now /naʊ/ 17

now and then /naʊ ən ðen/
17

number /'nʌmbə/ 13

nurse /nɜːs/ 47

o'clock /ə'klɒk/ 17

occasionally /ə'keɪʒənli/
17

October /ɒk'təʊbə/ 16

office /'ɒfɪs/ 47

often /'ɒfən/ 17

OHP /əʊ eɪtʃ 'piː/ 48

old /əʊld/ 32

omelette /'ɒmlət/ 53

on foot /ɒn 'fʊt/ 2

on strike /ɒn 'straɪk/ 60

once /wʌns/ 17

onion /'ʌnjən/ 43

only /'əʊnli/ 15

open /'əʊpən/ 42

orange /'ɒrɪndʒ/ 43

orange juice /'ɒrɪndʒ
dʒuːs/ 53

order /'ɔːdə/ 53

ordinary-looking /'ɔːdənri
lʊkɪŋ/ 32

out /aʊt/ 18

out of order /aʊt əv 'ɔːdə/
42, 59

outside line /'aʊtsaɪd 'laɪn/
52

overweight /əʊvə'weɪt/ 32

p.m. /piː 'em/ 16

package holiday /'pækɪdʒ
'hɒlədeɪ/ 50

pain /peɪn/ 30

painless /'peɪnləs/ 26

pair of glasses /peə əv
    glɑːsɪz/ jeans /dʒiːnz/
    shorts /ʃɔːts/ etc. 31
paper clip /'peɪpə klɪp/ 48
parents /'peərənts/ 28, 29
park /pɑːk/ 38
parrot /'pærət/ 40
party /'pɑːti/ 2, 3
pass /pɑːs/ 14
pass an exam /pɑːs ən
    ɪgˈzæm/ 48
passport /'pɑːspɔːt/ 2, 41,
    50
past /pɑːst/ 17
pasta /'pæstə/ 43
path /pɑːθ/ 39
pay /peɪ/ 20, 42, 57
pay for /'peɪ fə/ 24
pea(s) /piː(z)/ 43, 53
pear /peə/ 43
pedestrian area
    /pəˈdestriən 'eəriə/ 38
pen /pen/ 48
pencil /'pensəl/ 48
pencil sharpener /'pensəl
    'ʃɑːpənə/ 48
people /'piːpəl/ 36
perfect /'pɜːfɪkt/ 22
Peru /pəˈruː/ 36
Peruvian /pəˈruːviən/ 36
pet /pet/ 40
petrol /'petrəl/ 41
phone /fəʊn/ 12, 49, 56
phone box/number /fəʊn
    bɒks / nʌmbə/ 49
photo(graph) /'fəʊtəɡrɑːf/
    6, 8
photocopier /'fəʊtəʊkɒpiə/
    59
phrasal verb /freɪzəl 'vɜːb/
    11
phrase /freɪz/ 1
phrase book /'freɪz bʊk/
    50
physical education /'fɪzɪkəl
    edʒʊ'keɪʃn/ 48
physics /'fɪzɪks/ 48
picnic /'pɪknɪk/ 39
picture /'pɪktʃə/ 8, 46
piece of paper /piːs əv
    'peɪpə/ 48

pig /pɪɡ/ 40
piglet /'pɪɡlət/ 40
pilot /'paɪlət/ 14
pineapple /'paɪnæpəl/ 43
pitch /pɪtʃ/ 54
pizza /'piːtsə/ 43
place /pleɪs/ 18, 53
plain /pleɪn/ 53
plane /pleɪn/ 2, 14, 41
plant /plɑːnt/ 59
plaster /'plɑːstə/ 59
plate /pleɪt/ 21, 44
play /pleɪ/ 54, 55, 56
please /pliːz/ 13, 35
plural /'plʊərəl/ 1
police /pəˈliːs/ 57
Polish /'pəʊlɪʃ/ 36
politics /'pɒlətɪks/ 26
polluted /pəˈluːtɪd/ 60
pollution /pəˈluːʃn/ 60
pool /puːl/ 54
poor /pɔː/ 60
pork /pɔːk/ 40
Portuguese /pɔːtʃəˈɡiːz/ 36
position /pəˈzɪʃn/ 18
positive /'pɒzətɪv/ 23
possible /'pɒsəbəl/ 25
post /pəʊst/ 49
post box /'pəʊst bɒks/ 49
postcard /'pəʊskɑːd/ 10,
    50
post office /'pəʊst ɒfɪs/
    38, 51
potato(es) /pəˈteɪtəʊz/ 43,
    53
pre- /priː/ 25
prefer /prɪˈfɜː/ 34
preposition /prepəˈzɪʃn/ 1
present /'prezənt/ 9, 17,
    51
president /'prezɪdənt/ 25
pretty /'prɪti/ 32
primary school /'praɪməri
    skuːl/ 48
prison /'prɪzən/ 57
problem /'prɒbləm/ 59, 60
programme /'prəʊɡræm/
    56, 58
proud of /'praʊd əv/ 24
psychology /saɪˈkɒlədʒi/
    26

pub /pʌb/ 53
pull /pʊl/ 42
push /pʊʃ/ 42
put /pʊt/ 20, 49
put on /'pʊt ɒn/ 11, 31,
    59
pyjamas /pɪˈdʒɑːməz/ 45

question /'kwestʃən/ 1, 13
queue /kjuː/ 42
quiet /'kwaɪət/ 19, 27
quite /kwaɪt/ 27

radio /'reɪdiəʊ/ 12, 13,
    46, 56, 58
railway station /'reɪlweɪ
    'steɪʃən/ 38
rain /reɪn/ 2, 9, 10, 37
rainy /'reɪni/ 2, 26, 37
rare /reə/ 53
rarely /'reəli/ 17
re- /riː/ 25
read /riːd/ 20, 38, 45, 46,
    56
receipt /rɪˈsiːt/ 51
recently /'riːsəntli/ 17
reception /rɪˈsepʃən/ 52
redo /riːˈduː/ 25
relations /rɪˈleɪʃnz/ 29
relatives /'relətɪvz/ 29
relax /rɪˈlæks/ 46
remote control /rɪˈməʊt
    kənˈtrəʊl/ 46
repair /rɪˈpeə/ 59
reply /rɪˈplaɪ/ 13
reporter /rɪˈpɔːtə/ 58
reread /riːˈriːd/ 25
reservation /rezəˈveɪʃn/
    52
reserve /rɪˈzɜːv/ 41
restaurant /'restrɒnt/ 51,
    53
restaurant car /'restrɒnt
    'kɑː/ 41
retell /riːˈtel/ 25
return ticket /rɪˈtɜːn 'tɪkɪt/
    41
rewrite /riːˈraɪt/ 25
rice /raɪs/ 21, 43
ride /raɪd/ 14, 20
right /raɪt/ 1, 18, 19

ring /rɪŋ/ 31, 42, 45, 56

rise /raɪz/ 20

river /'rɪvə/ 39

road /rəʊd/ 38

roast beef/potatoes /rəʊst 'biːf/pə'teɪtəʊz/ 53

rob /rɒb/ 57

robber /'rɒbə/ 57

robbery /'rɒbəri/ 57

romantic /rə'mæntɪk/ 55

roundabout /'raʊndəbaʊt/ 38

routine /ruː'tiːn/ 45

row /raʊ/ 59

rubber /'rʌbə/ 48

rugby /'rʌgbi/ 54

ruler /'ruːlə/ 48

run /rʌn/ 14, 20

running /'rʌnɪŋ/ 54

rush hour /'rʌʃ aʊə/ 60

Russia /'rʌʃə/ 36

Russian /'rʌʃn/ 36

sad /sæd/ 6, 34

sadly /'sædli/ 26

sadness /'sædnəs/ 26

safe /seɪf/ 25

sailing /'seɪlɪŋ/ 54

salad /'sæləd/ 53

sale /seɪl/ 42

sandwich /'sænwɪdʒ/ 53

sandwich bar /'sænwɪdʒ baː/ 53

sandy /'sændi/ 26

satellite /'sætəlaɪt/ 58

Saturday /'sætədeɪ/ 16

saucepan /'sɔːspən/ 44

saucer /'sɔːsə/ 44

sauna /'sɔːnə/ 3

say /seɪ/ 13, 20

scarf /skaːf/ 31

school /skuːl/ 2, 47, 48

science fiction /saɪəns 'fɪkʃn/ 55

Scottish /'skɒtɪʃ/ 36

screen /skriːn/ 49

season /'siːzn/ 16

seat /siːt/ 41

second /'sekənd/ 16, 51

secretary /'sekrətri/ 5, 9, 47

see /siː/ 7, 55, 56

see you soon /siː jə 'suːn/ 35

selfish /'selfɪʃ/ 23

self-service (café/restaurant) /self 'sɜːvɪs (/'kæfeɪ/ 'restrɒnt/) 53

sell /sel/ 20, 57

send /send/ 49

sentence /'sentəns/ 1

September /sep'tembə/ 16

shampoo /ʃæm'puː/ 45

sheep /ʃiːp/ 40

shelf /ʃelf/ 44, 45

shine /ʃaɪn/ 20, 37

ship /ʃɪp/ 14, 41

shirt /ʃɜːt/ 31

shoe /ʃuː/ 21, 31, 51

shoot /ʃuːt/ 20

shop /ʃɒp/ 38, 47, 51

shop assistant /ʃɒp ə'sɪstənt/ 47, 51

shoplifter /'ʃɒplɪftə/ 57

shoplifting /'ʃɒplɪftɪŋ/ 57

shopping /ʃɒpɪŋ/ 51

short /ʃɔːt/ 32

shorts /ʃɔːts/ 31

shoulder /'ʃəʊldə/ 30

shower /'ʃaʊə/ 2, 3, 12, 45, 52

shut /ʃʌt/ 20

sick /sɪk/ 33

side /saɪd/ 18, 30

sign /saɪn/ 38, 52

single /'sɪŋgəl/ 28

single room /sɪŋgəl 'ruːm/ 52

single ticket /sɪŋgəl 'tɪkɪt/ 41

singular /'sɪŋgjələ/ 1

sink /sɪŋk/ 44

sister /'sɪstə/ 29

size /saɪz/ 51

skiing /'skiːɪŋ/ 54

skin /skɪn/ 30, 32

skirt /skɜːt/ 31

sleep /sliːp/ 20, 35, 56

slim /slɪm/ 32

slow /sləʊ/ 19

slowly /'sləʊli/ 26

snack /snæk/ 53

snake /sneɪk/ 40

snow /snəʊ/ 2, 37

snowstorm /'snəʊstɔːm/ 60

snowy /'snəʊi/ 37

so /səʊ/ 15

soap /səʊp/ 45, 51, 58

soap opera /'səʊp ɒprə/ 58

soccer /'sɒkə/ 54

sociology /səʊʃi'ɒlədʒi/ 26

socks /sɒks/ 31

sofa /'səʊfə/ 46

sometimes /'sʌmtaɪmz/ 17

son /sʌn/ 29

soon /suːn/ 17

sorry /'sɒri/ 35

soup /suːp/ 53

South America /saʊθ ə'merɪkə/ 36

souvenir /suːvə'nɪə/ 51

spaghetti /spə'geti/ 21

Spain /speɪn/ 36

Spanish /'spænɪʃ/ 36

speak /spiːk/ 13, 20, 49, 50

spend /spend/ 20

spoon /spuːn/ 2, 44

sports /spɔːts/ 54, 58

sports equipment /spɔːts ɪ'kwɪpmənt/ 51

spring /sprɪŋ/ 16

square /skweə/ 38

stamp /stæmp/ 10, 49, 51

stand /stænd/ 20

starter /'staːtə/ 53

stationery /'steɪʃənri/ 51

stay /steɪ/ 56

steak /steɪk/ 53

steal /stiːl/ 20, 57

steward /'stjuːəd/ 41

stomach /'stʌmək/ 30

stop /stɒp/ 41

storm /stɔːm/ 37

story /'stɔːri/ 13

strawberry (-ies) /'strɔːbəri(z)/ 43, 53

street /striːt/ 38

stress /stres/ 33

strike /straɪk/ 60

student /'stjuːdənt/ 2, 5, 48

studies /ˈstʌdiz/ 10
study /ˈstʌdi/ 48
stupid /ˈstjuːpɪd/ 23
subject /ˈsʌbdʒɪkt/ 48
sugar /ˈʃʊɡə/ 21
suit /suːt/ 31
suitcase /ˈsuːtkeɪs/ 2
summer /ˈsʌmə/ 16
sun /sʌn/ 2, 37
Sunday /ˈsʌndeɪ/ 16
sunglasses /ˈsʌnɡlɑːsɪz/ 51
sunny /ˈsʌni/ 26, 37
supermarket
    /ˈsuːpəmɑːkɪt/ 31
supper /ˈsʌpə/ 6
surprised /səˈpraɪzd/ 34
sweater /ˈswetə/ 31
Swedish /ˈswiːdɪʃ/ 36
swim /swɪm/ 3, 14, 20
swimmer /ˈswɪmə/ 26
swimming /ˈswɪmɪŋ/ 54
Swiss /swɪs/ 36
switch /swɪtʃ/ 46
switch on /ˈswɪtʃ ɒn/ 46
Switzerland /ˈswɪtsələnd/
    36

table tennis /ˈteɪbəl ˈtenɪs/
    54
table /ˈteɪbəl/ 46
take /teɪk/ 8, 9, 14, 20, 57
take … for a walk /teɪk
    fər ə ˈwɔːk/ 40
take a message /teɪk ə
    ˈmesɪdʒ/ 49
take an exam /teɪk ən
    ɪɡˈzæm/ 48
take notes /teɪk ˈnəʊts/ 48
take off /teɪk ɒf/ 11, 31,
    41
talk /tɔːk/ 13, 56
talk show /ˈtɔːk ʃəʊ/ 58
tall /tɔːl/ 2, 32
tap /tæp/ 44
tape /teɪp/ 56
tape recorder /ˈteɪp
    rɪkɔːdə/ 48
taxi /ˈtæksi/ 10, 14, 41
tea /tiː/ 3, 6, 21, 43
tea-towel /ˈtiː taʊəl/ 44
teach /tiːtʃ/ 20, 48

teacher /ˈtiːtʃə/ 2, 5, 47, 48
teapot /ˈtiːpɒt/ 44
technical drawing
    /teknɪkəl ˈdrɔːɪŋ/ 48
teenage /ˈtiːneɪdʒ/ 58
teeth /tiːθ/ 30
telephone (phone)
    /ˈtelɪfəʊn/ 12, 13, 49,
    52, 56
telephone number
    /ˈtelɪfəʊn ˈnʌmbə/ 49
television (TV) /ˈtelɪvɪʒən/
    12, 46, 52, 55, 56, 58
tell /tel/ 20
temperature /ˈtemprətʃə/ 2
tennis /ˈtenɪs/ 54
terrible /ˈterəbəl/ 22
terrorism /ˈterərɪzəm/ 57
terrorist /ˈterərɪst/ 57
textbook /ˈtekstbʊk/ 48
Thai /taɪ/ 36
Thailand /ˈtaɪlænd/ 36
than /ðæn/ðən/ 15
thank for /ˈθæŋk fɔː/ 24
thank you /ˈθæŋk jə/ 13,
    35
thanks /ˈθæŋks/ 35
then /ðen/ 17
there /ðeə/ 7, 9 10, 18
thin /θɪn/ 32
think /θɪŋk/ 20
think about/of /ˈθɪŋk
    əbaʊt/əv/ 24
third /θɜːd/ 51
thirsty /ˈθɜːsti/ 34
though /ðəʊ/ 15
throw /θrəʊ/ 20
thumb /θʌm/ 30
thunder /ˈθʌndə/ 37
thunderstorm
    /ˈθʌndəstɔːm/ 37
thundery /ˈθʌndəri/ 37
Thursday /ˈθɜːzdeɪ/ 16
ticket /ˈtɪkɪt/ 2, 41
tidy /ˈtaɪdi/ 59
tie /taɪ/ 31
tiger /ˈtaɪɡə/ 40
tights /taɪts/ 31
time /taɪm/ 13
timetable /ˈtaɪmteɪbəl/ 41
tin opener /ˈtɪn əʊpnə/ 26

tired /taɪəd/ 6, 10, 34
today /təˈdeɪ/ 16
toe /təʊ/ 30
toilet /ˈtɔɪlət/ 42, 45
tomato /təˈmɑːtəʊ/ 43
tomorrow /təˈmɒrəʊ/ 9, 16
too /tuː/ 15
too much /tuː ˈmʌtʃ/ 59
tooth /tuːθ/ 30
toothache /ˈtuːθeɪk/ 33
toothbrush /ˈtuːθbrʌʃ/ 45
toothpaste /ˈtuːθpeɪst/ 45,
    51
top /tɒp/ 18
tortoise /ˈtɔːtəs/ 40
tourist (information) office
    /ˈtʊərɪst (ɪnfəˈmeɪʃn)
    ˈɒfɪs/ 38, 50
towel /ˈtaʊəl/ 45
town /taʊn/ 38, 39
town hall /taʊn ˈhɔːl/ 38
toys /tɔɪz/ 51
toy shop /ˈtɔɪ ʃɒp/ 51
traffic /ˈtræfɪk/ 21
traffic jam /ˈtræfɪk dʒæm/
    60
train /treɪn/ 2, 14, 38, 41,
    50
trainers /ˈtreɪnəz/ 31
transport /ˈtrænspɔːt/ 14,
    41
travel /ˈtrævəl/ 2, 21
traveller /ˈtrævələ/ 26
traveller's cheque
    /ˈtrævələz tʃek/ 50, 52
travelling /ˈtrævəlɪŋ/ 41
tropical /ˈtrɒpɪkəl/ 33
trousers /ˈtraʊzəz/ 31
try on /ˈtraɪ ɒn/ 51
t-shirt /ˈtiː ʃɜːt/ 31
Tuesday /ˈtjuːzdeɪ/ 16
Turkey /ˈtɜːki/ 36
Turkish /ˈtɜːkɪʃ/ 36
turn down /tɜːn daʊn/ 11
turn off /tɜːn ɒf/ 11, 13,
    45, 46
turn on /tɜːn ɒn/ 11, 46
turn up /tɜːn ʌp/ 11
TV (television) /tiːˈviː/ 12,
    46, 55, 56, 58
twice /twaɪs/ 17

ugly /'ʌgli/ 32

umbrella /ʌm'brelə/ 8, 9, 31

uncle /'ʌŋkəl/ 29

uncountable /ʌn'kaʊntəbəl/ 21

under /'ʌndə/ 2, 46

underground /'ʌndəgraʊnd/ 14, 41

understand /ʌndə'stænd/ 20

unemployed /ʌnɪm'plɔɪd/ 60

unfinished /ʌn'fɪnɪʃt/ 25

unfriendly /ʌn'frendli/ 19

unhappy /ʌn'hæpi/ 23, 25

United States of America /jə'naɪtɪd 'steɪts əv ə'merɪkə/ (USA) /juː es 'eɪ/ 36

university /juːnɪ'vɜːsəti/ 48

unread /ʌn'red/ 25

unsafe /ʌn'seɪf/ 25

untidy /ʌn'taɪdi/ 59

upset /ʌp'set/ 34

upstairs /ʌp'steəz/ 45

USA /juː es 'eɪ/ 36

used to /'juːs tə/ 12, 24

useful /'juːsfəl/ 26

useless /'juːsləs/ 26

usually /'juːʒəli/ 12, 17

vandal /'vændəl/ 57

vandalism /'vændəlɪzəm/ 57

vegetable(s) /'vedʒtəbəl(z)/ 43, 53, 56

verb /vɜːb/ 1

video /'vɪdiəʊ/ 48

video recorder /'vɪdiəʊ rɪ'kɔːdə/ 48

Vietnamese /vjetnə'miːz/ 36

village /'vɪlɪdʒ/ 39

visa /'viːzə/ 50

volleyball /'vɒlibɔːl/ 54

waist /weɪst/ 30

wait /weɪt/ 24, 27

waiter /'weɪtə/ 47

wake /weɪk/ 20

wake up /weɪk 'ʌp/ 45

walk /wɔːk/ 4, 14, 42

walking holiday /wɔːkɪŋ hɒlədeɪ/ 50

want /wɒnt/ 34

war /wɔː/ 60

wardrobe /'wɔːdrəʊb/ 45

warm /wɔːm/ 2, 34

wash /wɒʃ/ 30

washing-up liquid /wɒʃɪŋ 'ʌp lɪkwɪd/ 44

wastebin /'weɪst bɪn/ 44

watch /wɒtʃ/ 12, 31, 55, 56

water /'wɔːtə/ 8, 21, 59

way /weɪ/ 13, 19

way in /weɪ 'ɪn/ 42

way out /weɪ 'aʊt/ 42

WC /dʌbəljuː'siː/ 42

wear /weə/ 20, 31

weather /'weðə/ 2, 21, 37

wedding /'wedɪŋ/ 28

Wednesday /'wenzdeɪ/ 6

week /wiːk/ 16

weekend /wiːk'end/ 16

weigh /weɪ/ 28

weight /weɪt/ 32

well /wel/ 10, 19, 33, 34

well-behaved /wel bɪ'heɪvd/ 23

well-done /wel 'dʌn/ 53

western /'westən/ 55

wet /wet/ 2, 10, 37

what time...? /wɒt 'taɪm/ 12

what's on...? /wɒts 'ɒn 55

wheel /wiːl/ 2

when /wen/ 15

widowed /'wɪdəʊd/ 28

wife /waɪf/ 25

wild animal /waɪld 'ænɪməl/ 40

wildlife /'waɪldlaɪf/ 39

win /wɪn/ 20

wind /wɪnd/ 37

window /'wɪndəʊ/ 2, 46

windscreen /'wɪnskriːn/ 2

windy /'wɪndi/ 37

wine /waɪn/ 43

wine list /'waɪn lɪst/ 53

winter /'wɪntə/ 16

winter holiday /wɪntə 'hɒlədeɪ/ 50

women /'wɪmɪn/ 42, 58

wonderful /'wʌndəfəl/ 22, 23

wood /wʊd/ 39

wool /wʊl/ 40

word /wɜːd/ 1

word processor /'wɜːd 'prəʊsesə/ 26

work /wɜːk/ 12, 21, 47, 59

worker /'wɜːkə/ 26

worktop /'wɜːktɒp/ 44

worse /wɜːs/ 22

worst /wɜːst/ 22

write /raɪt/ 12, 20

wrong /rɒŋ/ 19

year /jɪə/ 16

yesterday /'jestədeɪ/ 16

young /jʌŋ/ 32

zoo /zuː/ 40

zoology /zuˈɒlədʒi/ 26